JEWS AMONG ARABS

JEWS AMONG ARABS

Contacts and Boundaries

Mark R. Cohen and Abraham L. Udovitch
Editors

THE DARWIN PRESS, INC.
PRINCETON, NEW JERSEY

Library of Congress Cataloging in Publication Data

Jews among Arabs: contacts and boundaries / Mark R. Cohen and A. L. Udovitch, editors.
p. cm.
Papers originally presented at a colloquium, held at Princeton University in May 1986.
ISBN 0–87850–068–5 (alk. paper)
1. Jews—Arab countries—Congresses. 2. Arab countries—Ethnic relations—Congresses. I. Cohen, Mark R., 1943–
II. Udovitch, Abraham L.
DS135.A68J46 1989
961′.004924—dc20 89–23563
CIP

The paper in this book is acid-free neutral pH stock and meets the guidelines for permanence and durability of the Committee on Production Guidelines for Book Longevity of the Council on Library Resources.
∞

Printed in the United States of America

CONTENTS

CONTRIBUTORS

JOËLLE BAHLOUL
Indiana University

ELIE KEDOURIE
The London School of Economics and Political Science

DANIEL SCHROETER
University of Florida, Gainesville

SASSON SOMEKH
Tel Aviv University

NORMAN A. STILLMAN
State University of New York at Binghamton

LUCETTE VALENSI
École des Hautes Études en Sciences Sociales, Paris

PREFACE

During two days in May 1986 some fifty scholars, graduate students, and other interested individuals gathered at Princeton University for a colloquium entitled "Jews Among Arabs: Contacts and Boundaries." The conference was organized in awareness of the controversial tone in which the subject of "Jews and Arabs" has been discussed in recent years. Against the backdrop of the Arab-Israeli conflict, the Jewish-Arab relationship of the past has come under new and intense scrutiny, with historical questions often masking political predilections. Did Jews and Arabs live in harmony in the past as some claim, or did Islam despise and relentlessly persecute the Jews throughout the ages as is contended by others? We were not interested in entering into this debate.

Nor were we inclined to impose the traditional model on Jewish communities of the modern and contemporary Arab world, groups that now live mostly outside the Arab world, whether in Europe, the United States, or Israel. As Lucette Valensi, one of our participants, put it, the predominant theme in current scholarship about the Jews of Arab lands is "the road to freedom" motif, which emulates the theme of "out of the ghetto" and "emancipation" long prevalent with regard to the modern history of the Jews in Western Europe. It posits a trajectory leading from Arab oppression to liberation under the wings of Western colonial powers and European Jewish agents charged with the westernization and regeneration of the Arab Jews. This approach, essentially the approach of minority-majority relations, will doubtless continue to play a dominant role in future research, but it was not the theme that animated our colloquium.

Rather, the purpose of the Princeton colloquium was to examine the Jewish-Arab relationship from a different perspective. We wanted to explore the experience of the Jewish communities of North Africa and Iraq in the nineteenth and twentieth centuries as one example of interaction between a religioethnic group and the dominant surrounding Arab-Muslim society. To move beyond the perspective of minority-majority relationships, we hoped to examine the practical and symbolic exchanges between communities; the shared traditions and cultural forms of these communities; and their boundaries, which have served both as a system of communication and contact and as a means of separation and identity. In short, we wanted to explore the "Arabness of Arab Jews"—what it was and how it worked—and also to probe its transformation and its continuity in recent times and in new countries.

Accordingly, we deliberately chose the title "Jews *Among* Arabs"—not "Jews *and* Arabs," let alone "Jews *Under* Arabs"—to describe our endeavor. We hope that the six papers of this volume, which comprise the fruits of our colloquium, will make a qualitative though small contribution to a different kind of study of Jewish-Arab relations in the modern world, one that might be relevant for other minorities as well.

The conference was sponsored jointly by the Center of International Studies, the Department of Near Eastern Studies, and the Committee for Jewish Studies, with support from the Ivan F. and Seema Boesky Family Fund.

Mark R. Cohen
Abraham L. Udovitch
Editors

May, 1989

Lost Voices:
Jewish Authors in Modern Arabic Literature

Sasson Somekh

THROUGHOUT THE Middle Ages, the Jews of Arab lands did not participate *as Jews* in the mainstream of Arabic literature. The Andalusian poet Ibn Sahl al-Isrā'īlī (1208–51), for instance, does not reflect motifs and concerns that are specifically Jewish in his *qaṣīda*s or *muwashshaḥ*s, and we are always reminded by Arabic sources that he converted to Islam. There are a few exceptions, most prominent of which is Maimonides, whose medical writings and career received some acclaim in Arab bibliographic literature. However, most Jewish theologians, poets, and literary scholars who operated in the world of medieval Islam were rarely heard of in Islamic circles.[1]

It is a well-known fact that medieval Jewish writers in Arabic-speaking regions wrote profusely in Arabic, but they did so in Hebrew script. Some of them (e.g., Sa'adya in tenth-century Iraq and Judah Halevi in twelfth-century Spain) were widely conversant with Arabic literature and theology. Moreover, the language of their own Arabic writing was at times remarkably rich in style and far removed from the casual, semicolloquial Judeo-Arabic that we often find in the Geniza correspondence. Nevertheless, their literary production was meant exclusively for a Jewish audience.

As contrasted with, for instance, Christian participation in medieval Arab Islamic letters (e.g., Ḥunayn Ibn Isḥāq), Jews, whether by choice or by force, led their own, self-contained, literary life. Their Arabic works never came to be regarded as part of the history of Arabic literature. Parenthetically one might make mention at this point of the sixth-century Jāhilī poet al-Samaw'al b. 'Ādiyā', whose Jewish identity is acknowledged by the Arabic sources. He is lauded as one of the greatest Arab poets of all times. But then we are talking about the pre-Islamic era.

In modern times we find a somewhat different picture. Since the middle of the nineteenth century, Jews of the Near East and North Africa began breaking out of their isolation and exploring new areas of material and intellectual life. In a few countries (especially in the Levant and Iraq) they gradually became proficient not only in classical Arabic but also in some European languages. Here and there we come across a Jew taking part in politics and national causes. The Egyptian Jew Ya'qūb Ṣanū' (James Sanua, 1839–1912) was even known to be a member of the circle of Jamāl al-Dīn al-Afghānī, the famous Islamic activist; and it was apparently with the latter's blessings that he launched a series of anti-British journals. Furthermore, Ṣanū' was the first Egyptian dramatist of modern times and was fond of viewing himself as the "Egyptian Molière."[2]

Ṣanū''s theatrical activity and his numerous plays are in fact the first "Jewish participation" in modern Arabic culture, and contemporary Egyptian literary historians acknowledge his crucial role in the development of a local dramatic tradition. His plays do not reflect Jewish concerns, although the editor of these plays, Professor Najm, assures us that his dramatic works reflect Jewish social issues.[3] The life and career of Ṣanū' were exceptional in more than one way, but he was the only Jew of note who pursued a literary and journalistic career during the formative decades of modern Arabic literature. Another minority played a crucial role at this. As is well known, it is the Lebanese Christians who can be credited with the establishment of a modern Arabic press. They were also the chief translators of European literature into Arabic in the late nineteenth century and well into the twentieth. It was thanks to their efforts in Lebanon, Egypt, and the American diaspora that Arabic literature acquired many of its distinctive modern features.[4]

I now move to the twentieth century, in which the phenomenon of Jewish participation in Arabic literature and in the Arabic press became more pronounced.[5] This is true, however, only of certain Arab lands, especially Iraq and to a certain extent Egypt and Palestine. In Syria and Lebanon, in contrast, Jewish participation in modern Arabic culture is comparatively marginal. In the Yemen and North Africa, we find no such activity whatever, although in some North African countries a few Jewish authors appeared who wrote in French rather than in Arabic. In each of these regions the extent of Jewish involvement in modern literary life was the outcome of local conditions, which I will not go into here. Instead, I would like to concentrate on the two most active centers of Jewish literary life in our century, Egypt and Iraq. My remarks will concentrate mainly on the literary careers of two of the most prominent Jewish writers in these two countries.

Egypt

The Egyptian Jewish community in the last two centuries was not predominantly Arabophone; neither were its members entirely of Egyptian origin.[6] A sizable number of the Jews of modern Egypt settled there with the waves of immigration that swept in during the second half of the nineteenth century and the first decades of the twentieth. Many of them spoke languages other than Arabic at home (Ladino, French, Italian, Yiddish, and Turkish), and their communal schools were for the main part French-oriented. Nevertheless, certain sections of that community, especially the native Egyptians, imbibed Arabic culture. Certain Egyptian Jews were prominent in theater, cinema, oriental music, the printing industry, and occasionally the Arabic press.[7] This is especially true of the Karaite Jews, who constituted a substantial part of Egyptian Jewry and were well integrated into the local culture.[8]

From among the Karaite subcommunity comes the most prolific Jewish writer and poet of modern Egypt. This was Mourad Farag (Murād Faraj), who was born in Cairo in 1866 and died in that city in 1956.[9] Farag wrote mainly in Arabic, and while some of his books address specific communal concerns and legal issues, the bulk of his writing was meant for the general reading public and was most definitely regarded by him as part of the modern Arabic literature of his country. Three volumes of his *Dīwān* are proudly prefixed by lines of praise written by the leading Egyptian poet of the day, Aḥmad Shawqī; and the second edition of his book *al-Shuʻarā' al-Yahūd al-ʻArab* (Cairo, 1939) opens with a copious introduction by the Turkish-Egyptian scholar, Ismāʻīl Aḥmad Adham.

In fact, the very title of the book just mentioned, "The Jewish-Arab Poets," is indicative of a most basic theme in his writing. Throughout his long literary career, which spans some sixty years, he left no stone unturned in his effort to demonstrate the long tradition of Jewish-Muslim cooperation in the lands of Islam. The Jews are an integral part of Arab Islamic culture, he repeatedly asserted. They participated in the past in the creation of medieval Arab civilization, and they are willing and able to lend a hand in its rejuvenation. It is to be noted, however, that this theme received a somewhat different coloring in different periods of his life. In his writings published around the turn of the century we find pro-Ottoman sentiments and a clear interest in the Young Turks. The stress at that stage was on the Jewish-Muslim brotherhood.[10] Later on, his main concern shifts to the idea of nationhood, and the word *waṭan* (*patrie*) becomes central. The accent now is on the brotherhood of all Egyptians: Muslims, Christians, and Jews. In the late 1920s we detect in his writings a certain disillusionment regarding the prospects of national unity, coupled with a greater attention to biblical and linguistic studies rather than to public affairs.

A growing interest in the Zionist enterprise in Palestine also manifests itself in his poetry and prose of the 1920s and 1930s. He viewed Zionism not as an alternative or foreign allegiance, but most emphatically as being in keeping with Egyptian patriotism. He firmly believed that the two national movements, the Egyptian and the Jewish, could work hand in hand toward securing a better future for the inhabitants of the region. The dream of a Jewish-Muslim cooperation was therefore finally transformed into an idea of a possible link between the two national movements. Both movements, he felt, were his own. Three poems published in the third volume of his *Dīwān* aptly demonstrate his concept of identification with both nations. These poems were originally composed in 1926 to mark the Cairo visit of a group of Jewish professors from Palestine, a group that was given a lavish reception by the Egyptian government. The first two poems extol (in the traditional neoclassic fashion) the Hebrew scholars and welcome them on behalf of the Egyptian nation; the third is written in the name of the visiting Jewish scholars upon their return to Palestine and opens with the following hemistich: "Was it Egypt that we visited or was it paradise?" [*'afī-l-firdawsi kunnā am bi-miṣrā*].[11]

No wonder, then, that in subsequent years the growing hostility of Egypt toward Zionism and Egyptian involvement in Pan-Arab affairs dismayed Farag and prompted him to abandon national issues for communal ones, such as promoting a greater measure of understanding between Karaite and Rabbinite Jews. In the last two decades of his life the flow of his literary production became markedly slower. He devoted all his efforts to the conclusion of his multivolume etymological dictionary of Hebrew and Arabic ("Meeting Points of Hebrew and Arabic")[12] and the translation of some sections of the

Hebrew Bible into versified Arabic.[13] His presence on the Egyptian Arabic literary scene became increasingly imperceptible, and at the moment there is hardly an Egyptian literary historian who is aware of Farag's unique literary legacy. In all he published some forty books on a variety of topics: poetry (five volumes), essays, translations, and philological and legal studies. It would seem that because of his preoccupation with Jewish affairs, his voice as a poet was lost in the context of Arabic literature. The vision of Jewish-Muslim cooperation that he so passionately preached was absolutely shattered by new realities of the Middle East, especially after the establishment of the State of Israel.

Let us, however, go back some seventy-five years and browse briefly through the volume of Farag's collected essays entitled *Maqālāt Murād* (titled in French "Essai sur la morale"). This volume, published in Cairo in 1912, contains fifty-five essays on various topics: literature, philosophy, language, moral and social issues, education, and so forth. The essays originally appeared in different Egyptian journals, including the epoch-making newspapers *al-Mu'ayyad* (edited by Shaykh 'Alī Yūsuf) and *al-Jarīda* (edited by Aḥmad Luṭfī al-Sayyid).

One essay, "The Struggle of the Motherland" ("Ḥarb al-Waṭan"),[14] deals with the interreligious tensions in contemporary Egypt and is of special interest to us. Originally serialized in *al-Jarīda* around 1908, this essay represents the young, ambitious Farag at his best. He is fairly optimistic concerning the possibility of an Egyptian nationhood based on equality and fraternity. He passionately advocates the adoption of a constitution under which Egyptians of all faiths can work together for the good of their country. However, he reproaches his Muslim countrymen, gently but forcefully, for certain prejudices that their language betrays. These prejudices are highly detrimental to the coveted national unity (*al-jāmi'a al-waṭaniyya*). For instance, a non-Muslim acquaintance is addressed as *Khawāga*, whereas Muslims are addressed as *Effendi*. This practice was prohibited by the Ottoman government, but much to Farag's dismay it was still in evidence in Egypt. Furthermore, Muslims refrain from using the word *raḥma* (divine mercy) and its derivatives in conjunction with a non-Muslim. Egyptian newspapers, with the exception of *al-Jarīda*, even refuse to apply the expression *raḥimahu allāh* (May God have mercy on . . .) in death announcements concerning non-Muslims. Likewise, Muslims would never address their non-Muslims friends with the locution *al-salāmu 'alaykum* (peace be on you). Some of them even concocted a special form of greeting for non-Muslims: *nahārkum sa'īd* (Have a pleasant day). "I am writing this," recalls Farag, "because the other day someone called on me and began to address me with *al-salāmu 'alaykum* but he stopped short in the middle, and corrected himself by saying *naharak sa'id*. However, he went on addressing other men with the full *al-salāmu 'alaykum*. I admit that I was mortified."

Farag vehemently denounces these discriminatory practices, dubbing them unpatriotic and a violation of the true spirit of Islam. He argues that they were based, in fact, on a misreading of the Koran and marshals a variety of quotations from the Koran and its commentators to prove his point. One is indeed impressed by his amazing familiarity with Islamic sources.

Iraq

Iraq was another important Arab center in which Jews were active in literary circles.[15] In a recent book about the rise of the short story in his country, an Iraqi literary scholar shows that the first modern short story to be written in the interwar period by an Iraqi author was "Shahīd al-Waṭan wa-Shahīdat al-Ḥubb" (loosely translated, "He died for his country, and she died for love"). It was published in 1922 in *al-Mufīd* and its author was Murād Mikhael.[16] The fact is that Mikhael (1906–86) was a prominent Jewish educator, poet, and scholar, who died in Kiron, Israel. Among other things, Murād Mikhael was the headmaster of the Baghdad Jewish secondary school Shammash. He published several volumes of poetry and prose; and in his youth he was a close friend and disciple of the well-known poet Jamīl Ṣidqī al-Zahāwī. In the late 1940s he emigrated to Israel, and there wrote a doctoral thesis on the Geniza documents under the late Professor S. D. Goitein and also continued publishing literary works in Arabic.[17]

Mikhael was by no means the only Jewish author in modern Iraq. In the interwar period we find in that country a considerable number of Jewish writers, journalists, and translators of European literature into Arabic. In fact, it is possible to distinguish two or three successive "waves" or "generations" of such authors. The first generation made its debut in the early 1920s, and it included, alongside Murād Mikhael, such writers as Anwar Sha'ūl (to whom I shall presently return) and Ezra Ḥaddad (1903–72), who in subsequent years translated *The Travels of Benjamin of Tudela* into Arabic. A second generation came to the fore in the late 1930s and included such authors as Shalom Darwīsh (1912–), Meir Baṣrī (1912–), and Ya'qūb Bilbūl (1920–). A third and final generation was taking its first steps when the war in Palestine interrupted its activity.

About 1950, most of these authors emigrated to Israel and other countries. Most who have pursued literary careers in recent years have tended to write in languages other than Arabic, for example, Sami Mikhael (1926—), a prominent Israeli novelist who now writes in Hebrew, and Na'im Kattan (1928—), who settled in Quebec and writes in French. However, a few Israeli authors of Iraqi origin still write in Arabic, including two novelists, Yitzḥaq Bar-Moshe (1927–) and Samīr Naqqāsh (1937–). Their Iraqi background figures prominently in their works.

A few remarks are in order here regarding the three generations of Iraqi Jewish authors. It is interesting to note that members of the first wave of Iraqi Jewish authors were by and large apolitical. They were Iraqi patriots, who earnestly hoped for the emergence of a "new Iraq," a modern, democratic, and open state. However, they normally refrained from dabbling in political affairs. Most of their works were published in newspapers and journals that had no distinct political coloring. Some of them launched their own cultural journals, but these were also distinctly nonpolitical. By contrast, the second wave was more involved in Iraqi politics, and some of its members joined those political parties that admitted Jews into their ranks (e.g., Shalom Darwīsh, who was an active member of the moderately leftist National Democratic Party).

The post-World War II generation presents yet another set of allegiances. They were divided between those who leaned toward Zionism and those who were attracted to communism (or, as Sami Mikhael put it on one occasion: There were those who opted for a short-range cure [Zionism] and those who sought an all-embracing solution [communism]). Obviously, it was the latter individuals who espoused Iraqi causes, and some of them assumed leading positions in the outlawed Iraqi Communist Party.[18] It is only natural, therefore, that many of the members of the last generation of Iraqi Jewish writers were at one time or another pro-Communist.

Another point worth making is that unlike the Egyptian Mourad Farag, whose literary output was marked by a distinct neoclassic style, the Iraqi Jewish authors were fairly modern. This is true of all three generations, including the first, whose members (thanks to the Alliance Israélite Universelle schools, which had operated in Baghdad and other major Iraqi cities since the second half of the nineteenth century) were exposed to French Romantic and pre-Romantic authors. Their writings were by and large far more individualistic in their approach and simpler in their language than the works of other contemporary Iraqi writers and poets. In fact the very title of the previously mentioned story by Murād Mikhael ("He died for his country, and she died for love") is indicative of the romantic-sentimental predilection of his group. The second generation boasts one of Iraq's first realistic storytellers (Darwīsh), as well as one of the first experimental poets (Bilbūl). Broadly speaking, they played an important role in the development of a modern Iraqi literature, and it is not because of their insignificance that most of them are today all but forgotten in their native homeland.

A third and final point is that unlike Farag, the Iraqi Jewish authors usually refrained from raising specifically Jewish issues in their writings. Even such a clearly autobiographical story as Shalom Darwīsh's "Qāfila min al-Rīf" (A Village Caravan) presents no distinctive Jewish features, and its protagonists are made to speak the Baghdadi Muslim, rather than the Jewish, dialect.[19] This would be understandable in the case of the Communists, whose interest was in all-Iraqi problems. But many of the members of the first two generations of writers were deeply involved in Jewish communal affairs. The fact that their Jewishness is hardly evident in their literary works can be explained by their desire not to project an image of a minority literature. Alternatively, avoiding Jewish issues might be ascribed to the lesser degree of openness of Iraqi society, which, unlike Egypt, was not ready as yet to tolerate a distinctly Jewish expression in the interwar period.

Anwar Sha'ūl belongs to the first generation of modern Iraqi Jewish writers. He was born about 1904 in the city of Ḥilla in southern Iraq. Early in his life he settled in Baghdad, became a teacher and a lawyer, and pursued a literary career that spanned a full half century. He stayed in Iraq after the exodus of its Jewish communities in 1950–51, but he too was finally obliged to leave the country in 1971. The last fourteen years of his life were spent in Israel, where he died in 1984. In Israel he published a retrospective volume of poetry[20] as well as a sizable autobiography, to which I shall presently return.

In Iraq, Anwar Sha'ūl engaged in a variety of literary activities. His books include poetry, prose-fiction, and translations. In 1929 he launched his own weekly cultural journal, *al-Ḥāṣid*, which he was able to sustain for ten years. *Al-Ḥāṣid* hosted many leading Iraqi writers and also promoted young authors, Jewish and non-Jewish alike. Anwar Sha'ūl was highly esteemed by his Muslim and Christian fellow writers and in 1932 was elected a member of the committee that was designated to welcome the Indian poet Rabindranat Tagore, who visited Baghdad that year. Owing to his presence in Iraq after the emigration of most of its Jews, he is lucky enough to be occasionally mentioned in Iraqi literary histories.[21]

He wrote his autobiography *Qiṣṣat Ḥayātī fī Wādī al-Rāfidayn* (My Life in Iraq),[22] after he had emigrated to Israel, and it was published in Jerusalem in 1980. It records memorable events in his life and literary struggle. I would have liked to dwell upon this fascinating book at some length. In the context of this paper, however, I shall have to confine myself to summary remarks concerning two motifs that are paramount in the work as a whole and that determine its literary structure: that of the author's self-image and that of the rise and fall of the ambition of Iraqi Jews to add their voice to the fledgling modern Arabic literature of their country.

A literary autobiography is never a spontaneous flow of recollections. It is a well-established literary genre, involving selection, organization, and focus. Certain episodes, especially those related in the opening chapters, tend to assume a symbolic value in autobiographies, often reflecting the author's self-image and life philosophy.

The first five chapters of Anwar Sha'ūl's autobiography are highly indicative of his sense of identity. Chapter 1 tells us that he was born in the city of Ḥilla, which he identifies as the site of ancient Babylon on the Euphrates. It is to that site that the exiles of ancient Israel were said to have been deported, and it was there that they chanted, "By the rivers of Babylon, there we sat down, yea, and wept, when we remembered Zion." Thus the author's connection with his biblical roots are forcefully evoked.[23]

Chapter 2 intimates that the author is a scion of Shaykh Sasson, the patriarch of the famous Sassoon family. Here the word Shaykh is significant, because it denoted that special type of Jewry that is rooted in the world of Islam. In chapter 3 the author discloses that his mother, who died shortly after his birth, was in fact the daughter of an Austrian tailor, Hermann Rosenfeld, who had settled in Iraq and married into the family of Shakyh Sasson.[24]

Further, in chapter 5, we learn that the author's wet nurse (Arabic *umm bi'l-riḍā'a*, "mother by nursing") was a Muslim woman named Umm-Ḥusayn. For fifteen months she breast-fed the baby boy together with her own son, 'Abd al-Hādī. The two "brothers by nursing" meet in Baghdad many years later, and an emotional reunion ensues.[25]

The author's identity as projected in these chapters is, therefore, that of a Jew with biblical origins—part of the modern Jewish people but retaining deep roots in the Arab Islamic ethos, an Arab Jew who is proud of being both Jewish and Iraqi.

It is significant, then, that the book does not betray a spiteful or bitter tone, although it was written *after* its author had to desert Iraq for good. To be sure, the bulk of the autobiography records fond memories rather than a sense of disappointment. The non-Jewish personages whom Anwar Sha'ūl recalls are mostly portrayed as positive characters. In fact the only unpleasant ones in the book are those Iraqis who were in one way or another pro-Nazi. The German ambassador in Baghdad during the 1930s, von Grobba, is singled out as a major factor in the deterioration of Jewish-Muslim relations; and the anti-Jewish pogrom of June 1941 (often referred to as the *farhūd*) is seen, here as in many other Jewish sources, as the beginning of the end of a community that had lived in Mesopotamia for three millennia.

Admittedly, the rise of modern Zionism and the establishment of the State of Israel proved to be detrimental to the dream of integration and harmony that Anwar Sha'ūl and his generation nurtured. But anti-Jewish prejudices, as is evident in this autobiography, antedate the involvement of Iraq in the anti-Zionist struggle. Thus the 1920 disturbances in Iraq were not devoid of an anti-Jewish element, although the question of Palestine played no part in it. Fascist and Hitlerite ideas were becoming fashionable in some Iraqi circles as early as the mid-1920s.[26] At times modern Iraqi intellectuals would reflect in their words and conduct some deep-rooted anti-Jewish sentiments. Anwar Sha'ūl records an incident that occurred in Baghdad in 1928: a Muslim writer and lawyer, Tawfīq al-Fukaykī, buttonholed him one day to express his admiration for a poem that the young Anwar had recited at a reception held in honor of a visiting Tunisian patriotic leader. Al-Fukaykī, however, added wistfully, "It's a pity, though, that you are Jewish"—to which Anwar Sha'ūl retorted, "Why 'pity'? I am quite happy to be a Jew."[27]

In the face of such sentiments, Anwar Sha'ūl's efforts to assert his Iraqi identity and his Jewish Arabness were bound to encounter some insurmountable obstacles. *My Life in Iraq* is a sad book, in spite of the basically sanguine outlook of its author. His poetry and prose written after his departure from Iraq still entertain that noble but elusive vision of Jewish-Muslim and Jewish-Arab symbiosis. Yet, his labor of love, as well as that of his fellow Jewish Arab authors in Iraq and in other countries, was unrequited. Their voices were lost.

NOTES

1. In the case of Maimonides, too, Arab writers often claim that he converted to Islam. However, the modern Egyptian scholar, Shaykh Muṣṭafā ʻAbd al-Rāziq describes Maimonides as "one of the philosophers of Islam" because he regards all those philosophers who operated in the Muslim milieu as "Islamic philosophers" (see his introduction to Israel Wolfenson, *Mūsā Ibn Maymūn: Ḥayātuh wa-Muṣannafātuh*, Cairo, 1935, p. 4).

2. See Irene L. Gendzier, *The Practical Visions of Yaʻqub Sanuʻ* (Cambridge, Mass., 1966).

3. Muhammad Yusuf Najm, ed., *Al-Masraḥ al-ʻArabī/Dirāsāt wa-Nuṣūṣ III: Yaʻqūb Sannūʻ* (Beirut, 1963), p. iv.

4. See H. A. R. Gibb, *Studies on the Civilization of Islam* (Boston, 1962), pp. 245ff.

5. For details about these authors, see Itzhak Bezalel, *The Writings of Sephardic and Oriental Jewish Authors in Languages Other Than Hebrew* (Tel Aviv, 1982), pp. 279–310; see also Shmuel Moreh's bibliography, *Arabic Works by Jewish Writers, 1863–1973* (in Arabic) (Jerusalem, 1973).

6. See Jacob M. Landau, *Jews in Nineteenth Century Egypt* (New York, 1969); Shimon Shamir, ed., *The Jews of Egypt in Modern Times* (Boulder, Colo., 1987).

7. See Sasson Somekh, "The Participation of Egyptian Jews in Modern Arabic Culture," in *Jews of Egypt*, ed. Shamira, pp. 130–40.

8. On Egyptian Karaites, see Rabbi Yosef al-Gamil, *Toledoth ha-Yahduth ha-Qara'ith* (A History of Karaite Jewry), vol. 1 (Ramla, 1979).

9. On the life and works of Farag, see Leon Nemoy, "A Modern Karaite-Arabic Poet: Mourad Farag," *Jewish Quarterly Review*, 70 (1980): 195–209. Nemoy lists Farag's dates as 1867–1955.

10. Articles expressing these sentiments can be found in Farag's book *Maqālāt Murād* (Cairo, 1912); as well as in many poems included in the first two volumes of his *Dīwān Murād*, published in Cairo in 1912 and 1924.

11. *Dīwān Murād* (Cairo, 1929), vol. 3, p. 48.

12. *Multaqā al-Lughatayn al-ʻArabiyya wa 'l-ʻIbriyya*, 5 vols. (Cairo, 1930–50).

13. The last of these was a translation of the book of Job, published in 1950.

14. Farag, *Maqālāt Murād*, pp. 200–23.

15. On the Jews of Iraq in modern times, see Nissim Rejwan, *The Jews of Iraq: 3000 Years of History and Culture* (London, 1986). On the literary life of

this community in recent decades, see Shmuel Moreh's introduction to his anthology *Al-Qiṣṣa al-Qaṣīra 'inda Yahūd al-'Irāq, 1924–1978* (Jerusalem, 1981).

16. 'Abd al-Ilāh Aḥmad, *Nash' at al-Qiṣṣa wa-Taṭawwuruhā fī 'l-'Irāq, 1908–1939* (Baghdad, 1969), p. 85. The collected poetry of Dr. Murād Mikhael was published posthumously under the title Murād Mikhā'īl, *Al-A'māl al-Shi'riyya al-Kāmila* (Tel Aviv and Shafā 'Amr, 1988).

17. Other authors who emigrated to Israel from Iraq and continued to write and publish in Arabic include Abraham Ovadya (1924–), Shalom Katav (Sālim al-Kātaib, 1931–), Salīm al-Baṣṣūn (1927–), and David Semah (1933–).

18. On Jewish participation in the Iraqi Communist Party, see Hanna Batatu, *The Old Social Classes and the Revolutionary Movements in Iraq* (Princeton, 1978), pp. 650–51, 699–701, 1190–92.

19. Shalom Darwīsh's story is included in his book *Ba'ḍ al-Nās* (Some People) (Baghdad, 1948); on the dialect of the Jews of Baghdad (the *qeltu* dialect) as well on other Baghdadi dialects, see Haim Blanc, *Communal Dialects in Baghdad* (Cambridge, Mass., 1964).

20. Anwar Sha'ūl, *Wa-Bazagha Fajr Jadīd: Dīwān Shi'r* (Jerusalem, 1983).

21. See, for instance, Aḥmad, *Nash'at al-Qiṣṣa*, pp. 237–51.

22. Anwar Sha'ūl, *Qiṣṣat Ḥayātī fī Wādī al-Rāfidayn* (My Life Story in Mesopotamia) (Jerusalem, 1980).

23. Ibid., p. 12.

24. Ibid., pp. 12–14.

25. Ibid., pp. 22–23.

26. Ibid., chap. 17.

27. Ibid., pp. 117–18.

The Break Between Muslims and Jews in Iraq

Elie Kedourie

THE JEWS of Mesopotamia lived in the country without interruption for two millennia and a half. Babylonian Jewry, it is well known, was the leading Jewish religious and scholarly center in postexilic times. Following the Muslim conquest, the Jews of Babylonia became part of Muslim civilization, the greatest numbers among them eventually congregating in Baghdad, the new Abbasid metropolis, where they remained an important part of the population. Indeed during the twentieth century, they constituted the largest group in the city, and Baghdad could be said to be as much a Jewish city as an Islamic one.[1] Their speech was, of course, Arabic—an Arabic softer, and thought to be closer in vocabulary and pronunciation to the Arabic spoken in Abbasid times, than that of the Muslims of recent centuries, which had come to be strongly influenced by the speech of the Bedouins. These, owing to the weakness of Ottoman rule in lower Mesopotamia, had been steadily infiltrating into cities, and specifically into their Muslim quarters, from the seventeenth century onward.

To understand the reasons that led to the exodus of this large, ancient, and well-established community in 1950–51, it is necessary to go back to the great changes brought about by the Ottoman *tanzimat* (reforms). Initially the *tanzimat* were a matter of military and administrative reform, but the dialectic of this movement meant that, sooner or later, it would embrace much more than the merely military and administrative. In the belief that a strong state rested on the cohesion of the body politic, rulers came to desire that their subjects should be involved in politics and should come to believe that government desired their welfare—in return for which they owed it their loyalty. This was, in brief, the doctrine of Ottomanism, which claimed that all Ottoman subjects were, or were soon to become, equal.

Such a claim, whether or not it became a reality—and, in the event, it did not—led to the most radical changes. The traditional status of a non-Muslim *millet*—with all its inbuilt inferiorities—was now ostensibly to be replaced by equality. The traditional society had been crisscrossed by communal barriers that were now, by the ruler's fiat, to come down, with every subject (or citizen) to count as one, and no more than one, interchangeable, moreover, with every other one.

One consequence of this theory, which rulers were increasingly disposed to incorporate in rescripts, constitutions, and similar documents, was that the political space became greatly enlarged, and the number of political actors increased, gradually but inexorably. This was an unfamiliar and potentially dangerous state of affairs, since the traditional estrangements and hostilities, endemic between the religious communities that made up Ottoman society, could no longer be mitigated by the barriers set up by the *millet* system and by the unpolitical character of the population. The increase of tension consequent on this is evident in many episodes in the decades that began with the publication of the first reform edict, the Noble Rescript of the Rose Chamber, in 1839, and ended with the two Young Turk coups d'état in 1908–9 and the disturbed political conditions that followed them until the outbreak of the First World War. The Damascus massacres of 1860 and the much less serious anti-Jewish outbreak in Baghdad in October 1908 exemplify these tensions. "Stories are told and believed," wrote the British consul general in Baghdad, reporting on this outbreak, "and it is more important that they were believed than that they were true, that Jews had abused Muhammadans and had even met violence with violence, and that in cases of altercation they had claimed absolute equality with Muhammadans. Such things were never dreamt of in Baghdad and it caused the more conservative people to think that the Muhammadan supremacy might be in danger from the Young Turks."[2]

The British occupation of the three vilayets of Basra, Baghdad, and Mosul in the course of the world war was to effect a veritable revolution in the condition of Jewish life. After the war, the British brought these three vilayets together in a new kingdom to which they gave the name of Iraq—a name somewhat incongruously borrowed from early Islamic history in order to signal the revival of ancient Arab glories. To head the new kingdom, the British imported a foreigner, Fayṣal, the third son of the sharif of Mecca. Fayṣal came accompanied by some Arab ex-Ottoman officers who had deserted to the sharif during the war. Originally obscure and of little standing in Mesopotamia, they now became the principal figures in the new state. They shared with Fayṣal a Pan-Arab ideology. This meant that they were not content with ruling the three ex-Ottoman vilayets, but rather that they would use the new kingdom as a base and a jumping-off point for the realization of their grandiose dreams. In other words, the new regime, once rid of British tutelage, would pursue an activist, interventionist, and hence adventurous regional policy. The new rulers, lastly, were Arab Sunnis who were set over a very heterogeneous population of Kurds, Shiʿites, Jews, Christians, Yezidis, and Sabeans.

Under the new dispensation the change in the Jewish condition in Mesopotamia, which had been under way since the beginning of the *tanzimat*, now became most marked and clearly visible. No longer a *millet*, the Jews were now a "minority." This term is associated with electoral and representative institutions, in which "majorities" and "minorities" emerge from the exercise of the suffrage. Iraq was indeed endowed with a constitution and a parliament in which the lower house was supposed to represent the balance of opinions and interests in the country, as these were reflected in the voting. But the logic of such institutions required that majorities and minorities should not be perpetual, since a perpetual majority will have no incentive or deterrent to prevent it from oppressing the minority. The new circumstances meant that the former Jewish *millet*, now the Jewish minority, was required perpetually to conform and give assent to the views and wishes of the majority. This majority was in any case the creature of the government, which was in a position to manipulate, to its own profit and for its own purposes, the new Western-style political institutions. Thus, for Muslim and non-Muslim, Arab and non-Arab alike, these institutions proved to be a sham, a mockery, and a cruel perversion.

When the British conquered Mesopotamia, and during the early days of the new sharifian regime, the Jewish community seemed secure and prosperous. By far the largest part lived in Baghdad. A network of excellent schools produced increasing numbers of well-educated graduates who found ready employment in commerce, banking, and public administration—particularly in the Ministry of Finance, the railways, the posts and telegraphs, and the port of Basra. Jews were also to be found in journalism, and in music, where many talented instrumentalists played a crucial part in preserving and transmitting the native musical tradition.

The British occupation, the mandate that followed, and generally the preponderating British influence were all commonly thought, by both Jews and non-Jews, to offer further buttresses to the position of the community. This was largely an illusion, since British commitment to the sharifian regime, and later on the desire to liquidate the mandate, took precedence over every other consideration. But even before the country was bestowed on the sharifians, it was possible to advance the argument that from a British point of view the Jews of Mesopotamia had no advantage to offer. Jewish support for the British administration should thus be disregarded as both self-interested and uncertain. In a paper that was probably written in 1919, St. John Philby, who had served as a political officer in Mesopotamia under Sir Percy Cox, declared that the Jews of Baghdad had lost no time in giving expression to their opinion of the Anglo-French declaration of November 1918, which promised the setting up of "national governments and administrations" in Syria and Mesopotamia. The Jews, he declared, viewed "with genuine misgivings their own future committed to the care of a national government, in which, at best, they will be represented by a small minority." The Jews knew that their commercial prosperity and personal freedom were assured under British rule. Their "clamor" for British annexation of the country or British citizenship for themselves supported the view of "British officers that under British rule alone could administrative efficiency and—as they see it—the happiness and prosperity of the country be assured." The tone of Philby's observations is most probably to be ascribed to his disagreements with the acting civil commissioner in Baghdad, Sir Arnold Wilson.

But it was not only that the Jews had become involved in jealousies and quarrels between various British officials. As Philby's memorandum further shows, an official could put forward the view that the majority was not only to be preferred to, but had also to be protected from, the minority. If, Philby went on, the Anglo-French declaration

> is intended to be anything more substantial than diplomatic *camouflage*, the Jews of Baghdad are out of court, while the British view, so strongly supported by them—supported by them, be it noted, for purely selfish reasons—is not supported by the history of our rule in India. That experience should teach us that minorities are by no means opposed to the principle of Home Rule and should warn us that the Jews in their turn may turn and rend us, the

moment administrative necessity compels us—as it will inevitably do—to legislate for the protection of ignorant majorities against their avarice and speculation. To be more precise, I foresee as inevitable the introduction of legislation to restrict the right of Jews to acquire land; what will the Jews think and say then? Will they not join in the cry for Home Rule—the cry of sedition?[3]

There was of course nothing to justify these remarks, ill-natured and quite misconceived in the parallel they drew with India. Philby himself shortly afterward ceased to play any role in the affairs of Mesopotamia. But whatever his disagreements with those British officials who were the architects of the sharifian regime and identified themselves with it, in this at least he was at one with them, that they too exclusively supported the Sunni Arabs from among whom came the leaders of the new regime. For figures like Miss Bell, Kinahan Cornwallis, Hubert Young, Bernard Bourdillon, Sir Gilbert Clayton, and Sir Francis Humphrys, the allegation that they wished to safeguard the position of the Shi'ites, Kurds, or Jews in the new state would have been a libel, an embarrassment, and an annoyance.

If, however, it was illusory to hope for support or protection from British influence, it remained true that until the end of the mandate in 1932, the new regime was both weak and under restraint. The Permanent Mandates Commission of the League of Nations (so different in its operations from the Trusteeship Council of the United Nations) exercised a real measure of supervision that the mandatory power took very seriously and that in turn set the tone of its relations with the Iraqi government and served to make that government more careful and circumspect. In any case, before the advent of Hitler, norms of civilized behavior were still widely accepted and made for restraint and moderation on the part of these newcomers to the comity of nations.

Though, as has been said, British favor toward, or protection of, the Jews was illusory, yet the illusion was nonetheless prevalent, not least among both Sunnis and Shi'ites. Owing to the circumstances in which the sharifian regime was set up, the Shi'ites generally, as well as those Sunni officials who had remained faithful to the Ottomans until the end, were imbued with bitter anti-British feelings; and those Sunni new men who had been given power by the British could not afford to show any less animosity to their benefactors. One of the stock accusations against the British, which became a veritable refrain in the political rhetoric of Iraq, was that they followed the maxim of "divide and rule," and that in order to maintain their power in Iraq they patronized and protected groups such as the Assyrians and the Jews.[4]

As has been said, the sharifian regime was by definition Pan-Arab. Fayṣal and the ex-Ottoman officers who took part in the Arab Revolt had looked forward to the establishment of a state embracing all the Arabic-speaking regions of the Ottoman Empire. This ambition remained with them. The new regime was thus always looking beyond its boundaries and, once British tutelage was removed, would seek to pursue an activist regional policy, in regard particularly to Syria, which was under French mandate, and Palestine, where the British mandatory was charged by the League of Nations with encouraging and facilitating the establishment of a Jewish National Home. Iraqi Pan-Arab policy would be regarded with hostility by the bulk of the populations, for neither the Shiʿites nor the Kurds relished the prospect of being swamped by Arab Sunnis in the Arab state to which Fayṣal and his followers aspired. And as the Jews were soon to discover, an Iraqi Pan-Arab policy meant that events in Palestine would have for them disagreeable consequences, which they would be powerless to avert.

Fayṣal became aware that the country he was brought to rule was overwhelmingly unsympathetic to the ideals and ambitions of his regime. In a memorandum addressed to some of his followers, written toward the end of his life, he described the fissiparous character of the polity—the fears and suspicions of the Shiʿites, the Kurds, the Bedouin tribes, and the non-Muslim groups—and emphasized the need for a fairer policy toward the non-Arabs and the non-Sunnis, one that would give them the feeling that the state was regardful of their interests, and would thus increase national cohesion.[5] But a policy predicated on these concerns would leave little room for pursuing Pan-Arab ambitions. As events showed, both in Fayṣal's lifetime and even more emphatically afterward, Pan-Arab ambitions, rather than the welfare of the various groups that made up the new state, had the clear primacy.

One of the clearest indications of the leanings of the regime was educational policy. The character of this policy became amply clear as early as the 1920s, even though British advisers were still there and might be presumed to provide a brake on attempts to make schools into forcing houses of Pan-Arab ideology. But the record shows that either a brake was not applied, or that if it was, it proved inefficacious. One of those who came with Fayṣal was a Syrian, ex-Ottoman pedagogue, Ṣāti' al-Ḥuṣrī, whom Fayṣal immediately placed in a dominant position in the department of education. Ḥuṣrī was a relentless centralizer, who desired to make the very mixed population of the new kingdom homogeneous and cohesive. He looked upon schools as the means by which to indoctrinate the young in the tenets of Pan-Arabism—the ideology calculated to produce the national cohesiveness that he sought. Thus he opposed granting per capita subventions to Jewish and Christian schools run and paid for by communal bodies, unless his department was empowered to carry out the same indoctrination in these schools. According to the indignant remark of one of his disciples, a member of the departmental committee that decided on the matter, subventions were being showered on these schools with "a horrifying generosity."[6] Once the mandate ended, the close control sought by Ḥuṣrī was soon imposed.

The same disciple describes in his memoirs how, in 1928, as headmaster of the Central Secondary School in Baghdad, he incited the pupils to go out and demonstrate against Sir Alfred Mond, who was coming to Baghdad as Fayṣal's guest, and how he himself joined in the march against this "Zionist criminal."[7] As these demonstrations show, Zionism was becoming an issue that could move the young and that could thus be used as a weapon in Iraqi politics. Here was a direct consequence of the political indoctrination that Ḥuṣrī pursued. Though Ḥuṣrī (and also Mushtāq) was no longer in the department in the 1930s, there can be no doubt that the politicization of education, and specifically the emphasis on Zionism and Palestine, was diligently pursued by his successors, such as Fāḍil al-Jamālī, Sāmī Shawkat, and other high officials whose membership in the Muthanna Club, dedicated to the promotion of Arab nationalism, is indication enough of their personal inclinations and official attitudes.[8] But it was not only an ideological legacy that Ḥuṣrī left in the ministry of education. During his period in the department, a number of Syrian and Palestinian teachers were appointed. As may be expected, they were fervent exponents of Arab nationalism and, more specifically, made it their business continually to put before their pupils the grievances of the Palestine Arabs: the oppression they suffered at the hands of the British, who were allowing increasing numbers of loathsome Zionists to enter the country and exploit its native inhabitants.

How disagreeable and dangerous the Palestine issue was to prove for the Jews was brought home to them during Yāsīn al-Hāshimī's ministry, which was in power from March 1935 to October 1936.

Hāshimī, one of the ex-Ottoman officers who came back with Fayṣal to his native Baghdad and soon rose to the top of Iraqi politics, was a forceful, not to say dictatorial, figure, who throughout his postwar career showed a determination to pursue an active Pan-Arab policy. During this administration, which proved to be his last, an insurrection broke out in Palestine following the Arab general strike in April 1936. Hāshimī allowed and facilitated the surreptitious despatch of an armed contingent to Palestine, armed and financed by official sources. It was led by Fawzī al-Qāwuqjī, an ex-Ottoman officer from Syria, then employed as an instructor in the Iraqi military college.[9]

Hāshimī also allowed open agitation on behalf of the Palestinian Arabs. This was carried on by various journalists, of whom the most extreme were Salmān al-Ṣafawānī, editor of *al-Yaqẓa*, and Kāmāl al-Dīn al-Ṭā'ī, editor of *al-Hidāya al-islāmiyya*, the organ of the Islamic Guidance Society. Also prominent in this agitation, in which the distinction between Zionists, Jews, and Iraqi Jews was not easy to discern, was Sa'īd al-Ḥājj Thābit, president of the Palestine Defense Society, which, like the Islamic Guidance Society and the Muthanna Club, enjoyed official favor and encouragement. These intemperate and malicious press attacks were not all. In September and October 1936, individual Jews were attacked and murdered on the street, and a hand grenade was thrown at the premises of a Jewish club, grievously wounding one member. Deputations were sent to the prime minister and representations made. But no culprit was ever caught, and in one case the authorities even attempted to accuse Jews of the crime. Such was the panic engendered by these attacks that, in an unprecedented gesture, the Jews spontaneously carried out a one-day strike on 18 October, when businesses did not open and children were not sent to school.[10] There is no knowing whether these attacks would have ceased in consequence or whether Hāshimī, as is most probable, given the thuggish streak in his character, would have taken no notice. Eleven days after the strike, however, he was toppled by a military coup d'état and left Baghdad for exile in Beirut, where he died the following year.

But it was not only Hāshimī who was keen on making the Palestine conflict an internal Iraqi issue. It was much too profitable for the politicians to leave alone. Pressure on the Jews therefore continued in various ways. Thus Anwar Sha'ūl recounts that at a meeting at the house of Senator Ezra Menahem Daniel (who belonged to a family of great landowners) and attended by the head of the Jewish community, Ḥakhām Sasōn Kheḍūrī, he was told that the authorities had suggested that Jews should, individually or collectively, publish in the press notices declaring that they were citizens loyal to their motherland and to the government's policy, and that they had no connection of any kind with Zionist activities. Anwar Sha'ūl objected that citizens did not have to prove their loyalty, but he was told that the authorities were insisting on such declarations. And the notices were in fact written and published over the signatures of various well-known literary figures. This of course could not be the end of the matter. Anwar Sha'ūl's public declaration elicited in turn an open letter from Akram Zu'aytar of Nablus, who was then in charge of Palestinian Arab propaganda and who was visiting Baghdad. The open letter approved of Anwar Sha'ūl's sentiments and pressed him to be even more emphatic in his condemnation of Zionism. On Palestine Day therefore a telegram was sent, signed by various Jewish literary and professional personalities proclaiming their support for the Arab character of Palestine and the struggle in its defense.[11]

To place these events and those that were to follow in their context one has to keep in mind the increasing violence and thuggishness of Iraqi public life in the years following independence in 1932. The boundaries between the permissible and the impermissible changed very quickly. This was seen in the Assyrian massacre of 1933, when General Bakr Ṣidqī's troops, who had massacred old men, women, and children in the village of Simel, were accorded a triumphal welcome in Baghdad and marched in the main street to the tumultuous applause of the crowd. There was also open recourse to violence in order to procure changes of government—a method that politicians of all stripes felt no scruple in adopting. Again, as a result of Hitler's capture of power in one of the most civilized states of Europe, that which had been inconceivable now became a daily spectacle that the Great Powers of Europe seemed to condone. Before 1933 the fear that barbaric behavior would arouse the disapproval of the society of states had served as a restraining force; that was much less the case in the years after. To take one example: at the end of May 1939, Zu'aytar gave a long speech at the Muthanna Club in Baghdad in which he referred to the *Kristallnacht* as an example of the assertion of national dignity. He contrasted the great damage sustained by "world Jewry," as a result of a Jew daring to kill a German official in the German embassy in Paris, with the many examples of Jews treating Arabs in Palestine with such contempt that they were destroying them wholesale.[12]

One particular consequence of the disturbances in Palestine and of the Nazi war against the Jews was that the distinction between Jew and Zionist disappeared in Arab nationalist discourse. During a tour outside Baghdad with some Iraqi official friends in March 1938, Zu'aytar was taken to an "elegant house" to visit the friend of one of his companions. In the course of the conversation Zu'aytar attacked British policy and "the malignancy of the Jews and their plotting," and spoke of the necessity of working unremittingly in order to fight and destroy them. His companion interrupted to say that the host was not "one of them" and that his being Jewish did not mean that he was a Zionist. For his part, the Jewish host turned to Zu'aytar with a smile—the character of which we can easily imagine—and said: "Everything that you say is right. Please do not think that I am insulted by what you have said about the Jews, since I believe that the Zionist Jews will bring destruction on all the Jews of the world." "I was silent," writes Zu'aytar, "since when I attacked the Jews, I did not distinguish between Jews and Zionists, disparaging the Jews of the Arab countries without exception."[13]

The anti-Jewish campaign, spearheaded by people like Zu'aytar, spread in the Arab world in ever-widening ripples. For example, a Women's Congress for Palestine, which Zu'aytar initiated, met in Cairo in October 1938. The Congress was naturally meant to provide support for the Palestine Arab cause and to attack Zionism, but it also proved to be an anti-Jewish crusade. Thus Eva Ḥabīb al-Miṣrī, the editor of an Egyptian women's magazine, asked in a "distinguished" speech: "Will the Jews, who crucified Jesus in Pontius Pilate's time, crucify him again in the shadow of Balfour's promise, and will the British people which claims to love justice now become Judas Iscariot?" Nāzik al-'Ābid Beihum, from a well-known Beirut Sunni family, quoted the Greek Catholic archbishop in Haifa to the effect that the Jews who led Jesus to Golgotha and crucified him were now trying to expel his followers from his land. Mrs. Beihum also accused the Jews of wishing to rebuild the Temple on the ruins of the *Ḥaram*. Rāyā Jamāl al-Qāsim from Nablus complained that Palestine suffered under two greedy imperialisms, one British and the other Jewish. This latter "mighty Germany could not bear, far-flung Austria could not tame, the danger of which Italy with its vast empire felt, of which most European states have complained, and with which even central Africa has refused to co-exist."[14]

Zu'aytar, so active during the late 1930s in spreading anti-Jewish themes throughout the Arab world, had been among the many Palestinians and Syrians recruited by Ṣāti' al-Ḥuṣrī in the twenties, in order to carry out Ḥuṣrī's project of politicizing Iraqi schools and transforming them into an instrument of Pan-Arabism. Zu'aytar served in Baghdad until 1935, when he returned to Nablus and became one of the promoters and organizers of the Rebellion of 1936. He then had to flee Palestine and went to Damascus, where he took in hand the organization of propaganda for the rebellion and for the Mufti, under the benevolent eye of the Syrian government and with the acquiescence of the French mandatory authorities. When the rebellion was fizzling in the spring of 1939, Sāmī Shawkat, the director general of the ministry of education who introduced into Iraqi schools the *Futuwwa* modeled on the Nazi and Fascist paramilitary youth organizations in Germany and Italy, invited Zu'aytar back to Iraq, to take up the post of "national guidance" in the ministry, "in order to be a ploughman sowing the seeds of nationalism and of a noble mode of behavior among the Arab youth of Iraq." He was to take part in formulating syllabi and in choosing the prescribed textbooks (all textbooks had to be officially prescribed); and he was to serve on the committee commissioning these textbooks. Another high official in the ministry, Jamālī, also urged him to take up the appointment: his services were sorely needed by Iraq, and the minister, Ṣāliḥ Jabr, was insisting that he should come. Shortly afterward, Zu'aytar was appointed inspector of social studies, and a high official told him that his job was to serve as the watchdog—literally, the policeman (*shurṭī*)—of nationalism in the schools of Iraq. Zu'aytar was followed by a large number of Palestinian Arabs who had been fighting the British in Palestine, and who were now fleeing the country. They were all offered teaching posts, indeed given priority in filling posts. In this way the ministry became "a factory to manufacture fighters for the cause of Arab unity."[15]

Less than two years after the outbreak of war, the Jews of Iraq suffered a murderous assault that constitutes a landmark in their short history under Iraqi rule. The nationalist frenzy building up during the 1930s came to a head when army leaders, encouraged by the mufti of Jerusalem and the other Palestinian Arabs whom Iraqi politicians of all stripes welcomed with open arms, carried out a coup d'état and soon afterward became engaged in armed hostilities with British forces in Basra and Habbaniyya. The movement was snuffed out by British action at the end of May 1941; but both in Basra and in Baghdad, Jews were subjected to looting and murder by the mob, police and soldiers on the retreat after their encounter with the British. Basra city, from which the Iraqi administration retired on 16 May, was immediately looted, the Jews bearing the brunt of the disorder. British troops in the nearby quarter of 'Ashshar were under orders not to intervene. The policy of the British government, as the British consul in Basra explained to those who came begging for protection from the disorders, "was not to interfere in any way with the local administration or to occupy any quarter which was not essential to the safety of the troops." These orders had emanated from Wavell, who absurdly believed that this was the way to ensure British popularity in Iraq.[16]

On 1 and 2 June following, it was the turn of the Baghdad Jews. The anti-British leaders had fled a day or two earlier, and there was no government in existence. Looting and murder on a very large scale, directed exclusively against the Jews, followed, This was undoubtedly an outcome of the anti-Semitic preachings that had gone on for half a decade and more, and that Zu'aytar and his like carried on with the approval and indeed help of the government. As in Basra, British troops were nearby, but again as in Basra, they were forbidden from intervening. This prohibition emanated from the British ambassador in Baghdad, Sir Kinahan Cornwallis; the commanders of the British forces had been ordered by General Wavell to obtain the ambassador's approval for any directives they might issue. The heavy responsibility—the guilt—for what took place in Baghdad on 1 and 2 June 1941 has thus to be laid at Cornwallis's door. His reasons seem to have been the same misconceived ones that had influenced Wavell. But Wavell's orders had been given some time before the event and at a great distance from the field. Cornwallis, however, was in the immediate vicinity and directly aware of what was going on,[17] yet did nothing to stop the disorders. It must have been also at his insistence—for nobody else had such a power—that a crucial part of Wavell's instructions was abandoned, with dreadful consequences. Wavell had ordered that the force going to Baghdad should, once in the city, control the bridges over the Tigris. In the event, they were not guarded, with the result that on 2 June hordes of Bedouins streamed from Baghdad West to Baghdad East, the richest and most heavily populated part, and engaged in mayhem for many hours, without let or hindrance.[18]

There can be no doubt that this event, the *farhūd* as it was called locally, had a shattering effect on the Jewish morale and sense of security. In a report of January 1944, an assistant inspector general of the Palestine Police, while on a visit to Baghdad, called on Senator Ezra Daniel, whom he found to be a "courteous but rather disillusioned and tired man of about 67." What Ezra Daniel had to say does reflect something of the bitterness engendered by the *farhūd* and by what was perceived to be the British attitude to this ferocious assault on life and property.

> It seemed to him [Catling wrote] that the British were prepared to use the Iraqi Jews as pawns in their political game without considering the possible effect such a course might have on the Jews themselves. What had made the community especially bitter was the absence of any statement by ourselves condemning the murder, assault, robbery, destruction etc., which had been inflicted on the Jews during June 1st and 2nd, 1941. It was accepted, he said, that perhaps we were not in a position to compel the Iraqis to issue such a statement, but our own silence had been unforgiveable.[19]

A few months later, the British deputy inspector general of the police, Major Fraser Wilkins, also discussed the attitude and state of mind of the Baghdad Jews, and how they were affected by the events of June 1941. Wilkins of course had access, by virtue of his office, to a wide range of information about the attitudes and opinions of the various classes and communities in the country. In a letter of 8 April 1944 to the Oriental counselor at the embassy, Captain Vyvyan Holt, he ascribed what he considered to be the anti-British attitude prevalent among the Jews to their belief that the British had done nothing to protect them and had not insisted that the culprits be punished. There was a general conviction, wrote Wilkins,

> that the British Forces could have protected them from the mob attacks in June 1941, while the British Government itself did nothing to force the Iraqian Government to inflict capital punishment on the large number of murderers and looters, or to impose a collective fine on the City of Baghdad to be used to compensate them for the losses they suffered. This feeling [he concluded] is probably the strongest single cause of the fall in British popularity and it affects all classes.

This was an authoritative confirmation of the impressions formed by Catling during his short visit. But, in a despatch commenting on Wilkins's letter, Cornwallis endeavored to minimize, indeed to dismiss, the report. He declared that the Jews' antipathy toward the British was to be ascribed to price control measures introduced under British auspices—measures that had caused losses to Jewish commerce.

> These are [Cornwallis affirmed] a daily cause of exasperation and cause the Jewish mind to dwell with increasing bitterness on events experienced in the past or foreseen in the future which give any ground for a grievance against His Majesty's Government.

These remarks are reflective of Cornwallis's own attitude and mentality; they do not, however, throw light on the situation in Iraq. At the time, Cornwallis must very well have known—owing to the drastic diminution in the volume of imports and to the considerable monetary inflation occasioned by large British military expenditures—merchants were in a position to make, and did make, large profits on whatever commodities they had in stock or managed to obtain. It was therefore far from being true that "Iraqi Jewish commerce" was sustaining losses that could be ascribed to price control measures adopted under British auspices. In any case, from 1942 until January 1944, sugar was the only commodity subject to rationing and price control. And only in January 1944 were schemes for rationing tea and coffee introduced. So that the "Jewish mind" would hardly have had time to dwell on the supposed financial losses that price control might have occasioned, and the ambassador still less to fathom the mysteries of this Jewish mind. In any case, as the economic adviser to the British minister of state in the Middle East subsequently wrote:

> Neither price control nor rationing could be successfully applied in Iraq owing to administrative inexperience and lack of adequate control of supplies. Long land frontiers and shifting population made smuggling and evasion of regulations all too easy.[20]

One must conclude then that either Cornwallis was ignorant of conditions in the country in which he was probably the most powerful and best informed figure or—more likely—he was anxious to avoid, so far as he could, any recall of the events of June 1941 and thus any possibility of his being held responsible or blamed for what took place. In fact, immediately after those events, he had already sought to attribute their cause to "the unfortunate reactions to Zionism."[21]

At the Foreign Office, R. M. A. Hankey minuted Cornwallis's despatch: "Anyway we can't please everyone. We are reasonably popular with Iraqis at present and we must expect the profiteers to hate us."[22] Hankey's comment is a direct response to Cornwallis's views, which were obviously thought to be well-founded and authoritative. They were neither. It was pure illusion for Hankey (and his fellow officials, who shared his complacency) to believe that the British were reasonably popular with Iraqis. As events were shortly to prove, the events of 1941 and the occupation that followed had enormously increased anti-British animosity, which the official and intellectual classes had, in their impotence, continually nursed, nourished, and spread since the foundation of Iraq. Hankey's gratuitous slur on the Jews as "profiteers" was also directly inspired by Cornwallis, who meanly added secret calumny to earlier injury.

An illuminating indication of the atmosphere that reigned in the British embassy in Cornwallis's time is a curious passage in a letter written in July 1942, when Rommel's victories were threatening the whole British position in the Middle East. Freya Stark, the writer, had witnessed the *farhūd* and was then employed at the embassy as a propagandist: "You can imagine too," she wrote to her mother, "what a time it is for a propagandist with country seething with disguised Nazis and swastikas appearing everywhere (even on the back of my car). The people who are doing us even more harm that the Nazis," she nonetheless went on to affirm, "are the Jews, who are jittering."[23]

The end of the war brought the conflict in Palestine to the fore in a much more acute form, and this was to have immediate disagreeable repercussions for the Jews of Iraq. For one thing, the Arab League had been formed during the later stages of the war, and it quickly became apparent that the issue of Palestine was essentially the mainspring of its existence and activity. The members of the League were supposed to work in unison in order to secure the rights of the Palestinian Arabs; in reality they found themselves having, willy-nilly, to participate in an auction, each state being obliged to equal and surpass its associates in extreme demands and drastic measures. Before the end of the British mandate in 1948, such measures as these states had the ability to take consisted chiefly in boycotting commercial relations with the Jewish sector of the Palestine economy and in imposing vexatious and punitive restrictions on their own Jewish citizens.

The freedom of Iraqi Jews to travel was thus gradually withdrawn: the restrictions at first covered journeys to Palestine, then came to include the whole of the Levant, and finally, the entire rest of the world. Over time Iraqi Jews became more and more isolated, increasingly looked upon as hostages to be used in the conflict with Zionism, the targets of official anger or demagogic malice. In the economic sphere the apparatus of control dictated by the exigencies of war, which had led to greater centralization and to greater power being wielded by the authorities, by no means disappeared with the end of hostilities. On the contrary, the local governments took it over from the British agencies that had originally set it up and operated it. Exchange control, control of banking operations, and import and export licensing now became ordinary features of administrative tyranny. They came to be used both as weapons against individuals or groups who happened not to be in the government's good books, and as a new, powerful means for extracting bribes and benevolences.

The increasing politicization of economic activities took numerous forms. Thus we learn from Ṭālib Mushtāq's memoirs that in 1945 he was appointed manager of the newly opened Baghdad branch of the Arab Bank, which had been founded in Jerusalem in the 1930s by Ibrāhīm Ḥilmī 'Abd al-Bāqī, a follower of the mufti of Jerusalem. Mushtāq tells us that, in taking up his new position, he applied in Baghdad the principles on which the bank had been founded, namely, that no shareholder or employee should be Jewish. He engaged in a campaign inciting the government to boycott the services of Jewish banks; in this he was supported by nationalist newspapers. For example, on discovering that the government bank had transferred money to the Arab League in Cairo through an old established Jewish bank, Bank Zilkha, he criticized the procedure as being strange, against the public interest, and also in poor taste.[24] This was taking public anti-Jewish incitements to new heights, in a manner that would have been inconceivable even when Nazi influence over Iraqi politics was at its strongest in the thirties.

During the world war and in the years that preceded the establishment of the State of Israel, there occurred a new development, which was to have significant consequences for the fate of the Iraqi Jews. After the collapse of Rashīd 'Alī's movement, and the occupation of Iran, which followed shortly afterward, there was a great deal of British military activity, and Jews from Palestine began to be involved in providing services and in taking up contracts of various kinds for the British forces. They could thus move freely between Palestine and Iraq under British military auspices. The Jewish Agency took advantage of this state of affairs to send emissaries to establish contact with the Jewish community for the purpose of disseminating Zionism and encouraging and organizing immigration to Palestine.

In the wake of the *farhūd* of 1941 the young were receptive to such approaches. Small groups of adolescents and young men began to meet clandestinely, to be addressed and indoctrinated by the Zionist emissaries and to organize for self-defense and for illicit travel to Palestine. These activities continued after the war had ended and the opportunities afforded by the presence of British forces had ceased. As we learn from accounts subsequently published in Israel by those who took part in these activities, the Zionist organization in charge of illegal immigration was much interested in encouraging a flow of immigraion from Iraq. The reason, of course, is not far to seek. An armed struggle with the Palestinian Arabs was fast approaching; it was therefore essential to increase the manpower of the *yishuv* as much as possible. In fact the numbers of those recruited and of those who succeeded in illegally leaving Iraq and entering Palestine were both small, but after 1948 the unforeseen repercussions of this clandestine Zionist activity on the community at large proved serious.[25]

Another event, which occurred a few months before the outbreak of war in Palestine, also seems to have had some impact on the subsequent fate of the Iraqi Jews. In January 1948 an Iraqi government headed by Ṣāliḥ Jabr signed an Anglo-Iraqi treaty that had been under negotiation during the previous few months. The treaty was signed at Portsmouth by the foreign secretary, Ernest Bevin, and Ṣāliḥ Jabr, who had come at the head of an official delegation. Ṣāliḥ Jabr did not return immediately to Baghdad, and in his absence agitation against the treaty broke out, fanned by various politicians. Police clashed with the demonstrators, some of whom were killed. The regent, Abdul-Ilāh, had given his approval to the treaty but was weak, and Ṣāliḥ Jabr's rivals and ill-wishers browbeat him into disowning the treaty. This was a great triumph for the mob, and demonstrations continued until Ṣāliḥ Jabr, who had made a hasty return, was compelled to resign. As the British embassy reported, in excusing the regent's behavior, Taḥsīn Qadrī, the head of the Royal Secretariat, "made much of the rumours of Jewish firing from roofs on the demonstrators and said that a massacre of Jews was to be imminently feared." It is not known who spread these rumors. It may have been the nationalists, erstwhile followers of Rashīd 'Alī al-Gaylanī, now organized in a vociferous party, *Ḥizb al-istiqlāl*, in a bid to discredit both the regent and Ṣāliḥ

Jabr by showing that they were supported by the Jews (who were of course Zionists) and thus were traitors to the cause of Arabism.[26] And, to excuse his own behavior, the regent in turn invoked this rumor.

The rumor was a pure fabrication. Jews had no reason and no means to fire on demonstrators from rooftops. The only involvement in the demonstrations that might have been—remotely—described as Jewish was that of some Jewish members of the (outlawed) Communist Party, which, small as it was, took a prominent part in the disturbances. The activities of these Jewish Communists was also put to the debit of the Jewish community. Thus, Muṣṭafa al-'Umarī, minister of the interior in Sayyid Muḥammad al-Ṣadr's administration (which succeeded Ṣāliḥ Jabr's), declared to the British ambassador that he wanted to remove Jewish influence, much of it Communist, from the press. He had "recently sent for the Grand Rabbi and had invoked his assistance. He had pointed out to him that it was quite wrong that the Jews should be subsidising newspapers and taking such an active and objectionable part in internal politics. He had made clear the unwisdom of this from the point of view of the Jews themselves."[27]

'Umarī's allegations are quite peculiar. There were, it is true, some well-known Jewish journalists, but none of them was identified with a political party or a political position. These journalists were professionals concerned simply with news gathering and the efficient production of a newspaper. In Iraq, where official control of newspapers was meticulous and heavy-handed, they would not have lasted long had they taken a partisan position in support of a political cause. The accusation that Jews were subsidizing newspapers was even stranger. The purpose of such subsidies was to support a political interest, whether native or foreign. The government, political figures (all of them Muslim), or foreign powers did so; but Jews did not meddle in politics. If they were, perchance, to give money to a journalist it would be for him to stop making attacks on Jews, individually or as a community. And it was well known that some journalists did systematically use their newspapers as a means of blackmailing the objects of their attacks. But clearly this is not what the minister wished to convey to the British ambassador. His falsehoods are only an indication of the ill-will toward the Iraqi Jews that was brewing in official circles in the months before the eruption of the conflict in Palestine.

'Umarī's conversation with Sir Henry Mack took place a week before the British Mandate in Palestine came to an end. The Iraqi army, together with other Arab armies, marched into Palestine to prevent the establishment of a Jewish state. The outbreak of war in Palestine was accompanied by the proclamation of martial law to cover all Iraqi territory. Shortly afterward, at the end of June, the ineffectual Ṣadr vacated office and Muzāḥim al-Pāchachī formed a new administration , with Ṣādiq al-Baṣṣām as minister of defense in the new cabinet. Baṣṣām, an extreme nationalist, had been a member of the Muthanna Club and, as Akram Zu'aytar's diaries indicate, a fervent partisan of the Palestinian Arab cause. During his tenure in Pāchachī's administration, which lasted for only three months, the courts-martial were a feared instrument of persecution used against the Jews. But, as fellow ministers complained, the courts-martial were also used to advance "purely electoral interests." Two ministers, Muḥammad Mahdī Kubba at Supply and Dā'ud al-Ḥaydarī at Justice, clashed with Baṣṣām over this point and resigned. Another minister, Jalāl Bābān, at Communications, also clashed with Baṣṣām over the demand that all Jewish employees in the Department of Posts and Telegraphs be dismissed forthwith on the score that news about Iraq was reaching the enemy easily and quickly. Bābān demurred on the grounds that wholesale dismissals would disrupt Iraq's communications with the outside world. A violent quarrel between the two ministers ensued.[28]

It is not that the courts-martial had exercised their powers benignly before Baṣṣām took office. In his monthly summary for June 1948, the British consul general in Basra reported a "flagrant illustration" of the misuse of martial law when eight senior Jewish officials in the Port Directorate (where Jews were the mainstay of the administration), whose names were supplied to the court-martial by Anwar Mukhliṣ, the Muslim assistant port director, were sentenced to terms of imprisonment ranging from one to five years on the evidence of "highly unreliable witnesses" who had been collected by the same Anwar Mukhlis.[29] But Pāchachī's administration had been in office barely three weeks when the British embassy started reporting a crescendo of persecution. In a despatch of 14 July 1948 Sir Henry Mack wrote:

> There are two main trends to be observed. The first is a growing tendency to undertake a "witch hunt" against Iraqi Jews and the second, which is frequently combined with the first, is the use of military courts by persons in authority to make money or to pay off old scores. The Minister of the Interior [Muṣṭafa al-'Umarī mentioned above] is reliably reported to be making considerable sums by first instigating and then blocking prosecutions against wealthy Jews.

For some reason, it was in Basra that the operations of the courts-martial were most cruel and capricious. In the same despatch, Mack described how the *mutaṣarrif*, the assistant port director (Anwar Mukhliṣ) and the military commander (Colonel Ḥamdī Ibrāhīm) "have been working in close and sinister co-operation" and how their chief victims were Jews and members of the left-leaning National Democratic Party:

> Some of them were sentenced on the flimsiest of pretexts and the conduct of some of the trials was certainly most unfair to the defendants. In one case a man was arrested at 1 p.m. on one day and sentenced to a year's hard labour at 10 a.m. the next day. In another a witness for the defence was threatened, and in a third case, when a Jew was on trial and some non-Jewish witnesses were waiting to testify for the defence, the Assistant Port Director telephoned to the Court Martial telling them to expedite the passing of the sentence before the witnesses arrived.[30]

The picture of what went on at Basra is further amplified by the consul general's summary for the month of September 1948. The consul general speaks of the "unenviable" reputation of the courts-martial for "savagery and flagrant injustice meted out to Jews." He considers that the responsibility for this lay with the president of the law courts in Basra, 'Abd al-Qādir Jamīl, and the president of the court-martial, Colonel 'Abdullah al-Na'sānī:

> This latter [he went on] forecasts at private parties the sentences he proposed to inflict on Jews not even then arrested, let alone charged and tried.[31]

Sir Henry Mack humanely tried to mitigate this persecution. He went on leave in August, but his Oriental counselor, John Richmond, presumably acting on his instructions, spoke, and sent an aide-mémoire, to the prime minister about what was going on in Basra. Pāchachī declared himself sympathetic, and he did in fact send a circular enjoining the authorities to avoid acts "not in consonance with legality and legislative intentions," such as must obtain in a country "determined on forming a part of the civilized world, with its head held high and its reputation unsullied, the proper application of whose laws, and the correctness of whose administrative acts inspires confidence." But these high-flown sentiments availed nothing, for, as Richmond wrote, in Basra at any rate, little attention was paid to it. On the contrary, arrests of Jews continued to occur, and if there were releases on bail, extortion may have been the object. Also, Baṣṣām had issued an order that all Jewish employees in the Port Directorate, as in the Railways (and as previously mentioned in the Posts and Telegraphs) were to be dismissed forthwith. Even so, Najīb al-Rāwī, the acting foreign minister, could complain to Richmond that "Jewish successes in Palestine are making the Jews here increasingly provocative" and he was "seriously worried about the ability of the Iraqi Government to protect them."[32]

Baṣṣām reached the apogee of his career as minister of defense with the trial and execution of Shafīq 'Ades in Basra. 'Ades was a wealthy Jewish merchant who with his brother had established a prosperous car import business. At the end of 1947, the Jewish community of Basra had elected him as its president. In his monthly summary for December 1947, the British consul general remarked that it was probably unwise for the community to have done so, as the local branch of the Istiqlāl Party (comprising the prewar members of the Muthanna Club, the supporters of Rashīd 'Alī, and the most extreme Pan-Arab nationalists) was waging a campaign of anti-Jewish intimidation, and accusing 'Ades of smuggling arms to Palestine.[33]

'Ades was arrested in September 1948. On the sixteenth he was sentenced to death and fined five million dinars. The charges against him were as follows: that he promoted strikes in Basra the previous April; that he had financed the National Democratic Party (which was legally constituted and recognized); that he deliberately outbid the government arms-buying agency; that he had disposed of underground dumps of arms and ammunition at Shaiba (which had been a British base and where a great deal of army surplus was sold off to various dealers after the war); and that he had sent to Palestine for reassembly parts of tanks and other military equipment that he had bought from the British army disposals company at Shaiba. The defendant was not allowed to call witnesses on his behalf. As may be easily appreciated, the trial and sentence fell like a thunderbolt on the Jews. It dealt a great blow to their sense of security, the clearest indication to date of how vulnerable and how bereft of the protection of the law they had become. As an official in the Foreign Office, R. H. Clinton-Thomas, put it in a minute: the trial and sentence put the Iraqi Jews on notice that they were likely in the future to find little difference between the Iraqi government and Iraqi mob justice.[34]

Two days after sentence was passed, Mack saw the prime minister, who declared himself opposed to capital punishment, yet thought that "in the interests of public security, the sentence should be carried out." Pāchachī said that anyway, this was a matter for the regent, and in fact, as Mack subsequently reported, the government "ostentatiously" refused to take any responsibility for advising the regent. Mack then saw the regent, "who showed no inclination to discuss the matter." As Mack later explained, the sentence had been handed down by a military court, and the regent "apparently felt that the opinion and loyalty of the Army is of such importance to him at the moment that he could not risk going against the Court's decision." This was not the first time that the regent had behaved in this cowardly manner. On 1–2 June 1941, despite his reassumed powers as the commander in chief of the army, he had tried very hard to shuffle off on to others the responsibility of ordering the army to stop the disorders in Baghdad.[35] 'Ades was publicly hanged outside the British consulate general in Basra on 23 September.

Mack seems to have acted on his own, and in the absence of an instruction that he should press for a commutation of the sentence, there was little he could do in the face of the prime minister's and the regent's attitude. The death sentence aroused shock and protest among Jews in the West, and particularly in the United States. The Department of State was under pressure to intervene, and repeatedly instructed the ambassador, George Wadsworth, to make representations. Wadsworth, well known for his pro-Arab sympathies, felt, as Mack reported, "intense discomfort" in doing so. He did speak to the regent but heard from him the same apologia for his impotence: that for him to intervene would imperil the popularity of the regime. Presumably in order to excuse Iraqi actions, the U.S. embassy tried to portray 'Ades in as bad a light as could be managed. In 1943 he had been, they said, guilty of trading with the enemy, and in 1947 he had bought from American army disposals ten thousand tons of barbed wire, which he subsequently sold to a South African Jew. On this report M. T. Walker of the Foreign Office penned a minute. This world authority on Iraqi business history declared that there was no doubt that 'Ades was a slippery customer, that his name was an unsavory one, and that if the Iraqis wished to hang a Jew they could not have chosen better than they did.[36]

Though the prime minister was unwilling to intervene in the 'Ades case, he must have been shaken by the reactions to the trial and the hanging both in Iraq and abroad. He and other ministers decided therefore that the scope of the military courts should be narrowed. They wished to dispense with the provincial military courts and to have instead only one military court for the whole country that would sit in Baghdad and thus be under the stricter control of the prime minister. Baṣṣām objected to this change and resigned on 27 September.[37]

But Baṣṣām's resignation and also the changes in the administration of martial law do not seem to have appreciably ameliorated the situation of the Jews. At the beginning of 1949, the Board of Deputies of British Jews sent to the Foreign Office a long list of discriminatory and oppressive measures from which they alleged the Jews in Iraq were suffering. Their memorandum was sent to the Baghdad embassy, and commented on in a long minute by J. C. B. Richmond. The minute began:

> The Board of Deputies of British Jews are coming up against the difficulty which was foreseen when Zionism started by various responsible Jewish bodies, that is, that the success of Zionism would necessarily entail discrimination against Jews in other countries. British Jews who danced the Hora in the streets of London on the announcement of de facto recognition [on 29 January 1949 by the U.K. of Israel] and talk about the hoisting of "our" flag can hardly expect to be permanently regarded as loyal British citizens. *A fortiori* Iraq, an Arab country whose brother Arabs have been displaced to make room for the Jewish State, can hardly be expected to continue to treat its Jewish citizens as if they continued to be merely a religious minority. The question of dual loyalty now that the Jewish State has been established is bound to arise increasingly and the Jews should make up their minds once and for all whether they want to be a religious minority or the supporters of a Nationalist State.

Having thus made clear where he stood and how he regarded both his Jewish fellow citizens and the Jewish citizens of Iraq, Richmond went on to dismiss most of the charges preferred by the Board as exaggerated or false. But when the minute comes to itemize these "charges," it becomes evident that the situation of the Jews still continued percarious—despite Richmond's eagerness to defend Iraqi actions. Martial law had been used indiscriminately but the position was now "a good deal better," though there are still bad "cases": "e.g., that of Rubin Battat who has just been sentenced to three years imprisonment because of a judgement he passed in 1922 in his capacity as Vice-President of the Court at Basra which had to do with a charitable bequest by a Basrawi Jew to a charity in Palestine." Richmond could not confirm or deny figures of Jews alleged to be in prison, but a large number in any case were on Communist rather than Zionist charges.

Muṣṭafa al-ʿUmarī, the minister of the interior in Pāchachī's cabinet, was "strongly rumoured to have made considerable sums" out of bribes paid by Jews pursued by the police. It was true, again, that "efforts" had been made to eliminate Jewish employees from government service, but there were "some" Jews in government service. To allege, as the Board did, that "all" had been dismissed, Richmond protested, was an exaggeration. It was true, however, that newly graduated Jewish doctors were neither employed by the government nor allowed to practice privately. There were no general official restrictions on Jewish trade, "but I imagine Jews are having things less their own way" in trade and the professions than in the past. But there were still "plenty of prosperous Jews." No law had been enacted to confiscate the property of Iraqi Jews residing abroad, but "in certain cases Jews absent from Iraq have been tried by Military Courts and in their absence their moveable property has been confiscated by order of the Military Court," and so on.[38] Richmond's very eagerness thus to defend the Iraqi government and to paint the situation in as rosy terms as possible is itself an eloquent indication of what in reality was going on.

A month before Richmond wrote his minute, Pāchachī had resigned and Nūrī al-Saʿīd succeeded him. Martial law, with all its arbitrariness, remained in place; the same pressures and the same restrictions were still operative. One response to the situation, particularly by the young, was to try to escape to Israel. The Zionist network, which had been in place since the Second World War, continued to organize the smuggling of small groups to Iran, either through Basra in the south or Khanaqin in the northeast. These activities did not go undetected, and the police set out to discover and dismantle the network. This meant that those suspected of involvement in these secret, illegal activities, together with their families and associates, were subject to sudden arrest, detention, and frequently torture. In October 1949 the police arrested a young Jew on suspicion of being a Communist. He had a great deal of information about Zionist activities, however, and told what he knew. It is said that he accompanied police in their raids on private houses in order to help them identify the culprits. The wave of arrests grew wider and more indiscriminate, and the anguished relations of those arrested confronted the chief rabbi and demanded that he intervene with the authorities. An altercation followed. The rabbi was physically molested and had to be rescued from his assailants by the police. As a mark of protest against official persecution a fast was proclaimed for 25 October, and Jewish businesses and schools remained closed. The reaction of one member of the British embassy is curious and deserves to be recalled. In a minute of 23 October, John Richmond wrote of the possibility of a fast and a demonstration:

> If both items of my information are true, the Jews are heading straight for trouble. It is the old game of getting themselves persecuted to arouse sympathy and enthusiasm as when they stretched out their necks to the Roman soldiers in the arena at Caesaria.[39]

The Zionists were forced to dismantle their network and bring their activities to an end. Criticism of the chief rabbi, Ḥakhām Sasōn Kheḍūri, and attacks on his leadership of the community continued until he decided to resign, in December. He was succeeded by a well-connected and influential notable, Ḥesqēl Shemṭōb.[40]

These serious events, far-reaching in their eventual consequences, took place during Nūrī al-Sa'īd's tenure of office, which ended in December 1949. Soon after taking office at the beginning of the year, Nūrī and some of his colleagues began floating, both privately and publicly, a project regarding the future of the Iraqi Jews, a project highly indicative of the Jews' precarious position—now made untenable by the conflict in Palestine and its repercussions on the internal and regional politics of Israel's neighbors. The Iraqi Jews had no way of comprehending, let alone influencing these repercussions and the maneuverings they engendered. When the Anglo-American committee of inquiry visited Baghdad in March 1946, one Jew who gave evidence before it was Ibrāhīm al-Kabīr, the director general of the ministry of finance. He made the point that the Jews were not politically minded and had no political organization and no political leaders. An example of this political innocence was al-Kabīr's own statement that "it can hardly be believed that, unless the political system of this country is basically changed, the Jews can be singled out for oppressive legislation."[41] Some two years later, what al-Kabīr had dismissed as unthinkable was becoming reality.

Very shortly after assuming office, then, Nūrī began to threaten the expulsion of all Iraqi Jews (of whom he declared there were 150–160 thousand)—unless the refugees created by the war in Palestine were given proper compensation and allowed to return to their places of origin.[42] In April, Foreign Minister Jamālī repeated Nūrī's threat to an interlocutor at the British embassy. "To my suggestion that this would cause considerable economic dislocation," this interlocutor recorded, "he said they would import Scottish and Pakistani accountants and alleged that Jewish commercial influence had only been brought into Iraq by the British. Previously, the Shi'ite minister claimed, "the merchants had all been Shias." "Dr. Jamali," his interlocutor reported, "is clearly going to be very obstinate on this issue and will not listen to reason."[43]

At about the same time, Mark Ethridge, the U.S. representative on the UN Palestine Conciliation Commission, had a conversation with Walter Eytan, the director general of the Israeli Foreign Ministry, about the resettlement of Palestinian Arab refugees. The United States was then trying to promote this in various Arab countries through the promise of substantial funds for economic development. George McGhee of the State Department was the official in charge of this plan. He had been appointed U.S. Coordinator on Palestine Refugee Matters, and there was talk of a McGhee Plan to deal with the problem. Ethridge told Eytan that the British were to have a share in the execution of this plan, since there was no other way of persuading Iraq to take part. "When I pressed him a little further on this," Eytan reported, "I discovered that he had in mind a transfer of population. We are to take all the Iraqi Jews (estimated by Ethridge at 160,000) as promised by B[en]-G[urion] (according to Ethridge) and in return Iraq will receive 160,000 Arab refugees and 'McGhee aid' to finance their settlement."[44] Ethridge had in fact seen Ben-Gurion shortly before, but it is not clear that such an exchange was mooted. Ben-Gurion's diary, which gives details of the meeting on 18 April, is silent about population transfers or Iraqi Jews.[45] It is significant that Ethridge should mention the figure of 160,000 Iraqi Jews—precisely the number that Nūrī was threatening to expel from Iraq. Whatever the exact truth about his conversation with Ben-Gurion, Ethridge's words at any rate indicate that the Iraqi Jews were now being looked upon as a useful pawn for outside powers to use in their attempts to settle the Palestine conflict. There is further evidence that this was indeed the case. On 18 October 1949, Hector McNeil, minister of state at the Foreign Office, told Abba Eban in New York that "exchange, transfer, was best solution." The following day, McGhee in Washington asked Eliahu Elath, the Israeli ambassador, whether they were ready to admit Iraqi Jews even at the cost of additional economic difficulties. Elath replied in the affirmative.[46]

In July, Ḍiya' Ja'far, the economics minister, asked J. E. Chadwick of the Eastern Department of the Foreign Office whether he did not agree that an exchange of populations would be an appropriate solution: "If all the Jews in Iraq went to Israel," he affirmed, "Iraq would be freed from all its troubles."[47] A few days later Nūrī declared in conversation with Mack that if Israel gave up the territories outside the boundaries prescribed by the United Nations in 1947 that it now occupied, Iraq would "allow voluntary removal of Iraqi Jews to Palestine under certain conditions." Otherwise, Nūrī had in mind the compulsory removal of 100,000 Jews and their replacement with a like number of Palestinian refugees to whom Iraqi Jewish property would be given in compensation for what they had lost in Palestine.[48]

Now also for Nūrī and his colleagues, their Jewish fellow citizens had become pawns and hostages, to be used in pursuance of Iraqi ambitions in the Pan-Arab arena and to allow Nūrī to appear as the champion of the Palestinian Arabs. Nūrī was unremitting in his campaign. In October, the Economic Survey Mission for the Middle East, which was concerned with facilitating the resettlement of the Palestinian refugees and headed by Gordon Clapp, visited Baghdad. The deputy chief of the Mission, Sir Desmond Morton, received the impression that Nūrī was considering an exchange of populations and that he was willing to let the Iraqi Jews take their property with them. Morton's impression was erroneous, as the Baghdad embassy pointed out shortly afterward: whatever Nūrī had actually said or Morton understood, it was most doubtful that Nūrī had meant this.[49] In fact, a newspaper under Nūrī's control, *al-'Ahd*, unleashed an attack on the Economic Survey Mission, accusing it of attempting to bribe the Palestinian refugees to accept resettlement outside Palestine, and to rescue Israel from its economic plight. The only proper course, *al-'Ahd* proclaimed, was for the Arab states to boycott the mission. Also, referring to an alleged report from Amman, *al-'Ahd* divulged that Nūrī had told the Clapp mission that he was prepared to exchange Iraqi Jews for Arab refugees from Palestine. The Baghdad embassy reported that the press as a whole, and particularly the right-wing press, took up Nūrī's proposal with enthusiasm and gave it much support. The Jews, the newspapers declared, constituted a dangerous fifth column operating on behalf of an expansionist Israel. "The whole discussion," the embassy reported, "is being conducted on the assumption that the Jews' property would be confiscated and used to compensate the incoming Arabs for the loss of their property in Palestine."[50]

Nūrī's project to expel Iraqi Jews from their country or to exchange them for Palestinian Arab refugees gave the Middle East Secretariat at the Foreign Office (set up to encourage Middle Eastern economic development) the idea that an exchange of population, properly organized, might benefit both Israel and Iraq: "Iraq would be relieved of a minority whose position is always liable to add to the difficulties of maintaining public order in time of tension," and "Israel would find it hard to resist an opportunity of bringing a substantial number of Jews to Israel." The Secretariat hastened to add, however, that any idea of expelling Jews from Iraq should "obviously be discouraged." But both the British Middle East Office in Cairo and the Baghdad embassy were quick to point out the shortcomings of such a scheme. An exchange of population, the Middle East office pointed out, required planning and following very elaborate arrangements, which an Arab administration would be incapable of carrying out. The transfer, through inefficiency and ill-will, would become expulsion. The Baghdad embassy had an even more cogent objection. By putting such a scheme forward, they claimed,

> we should be virtually admitting the Iraqi thesis that Iraqi Jews have no right to be in Iraq. [This would] probably be used by them to support their ideas for the expulsion of the Jews and they are still thinking quite seriously that this must happen sooner or later.

If an exchange of population did take place, hardships for the Iraqi Jews would be inevitable; and if the British were mixed up with it, they would be accused of promoting the expulsion.[51]

The profitable linking of the Palestinian Arab refugee problem to the problem created by the Iraqi government in its treatment of the Iraqi Jews also occurred to some Israelis. A. Katznelson, a member of the Israeli delegation to the United Nations General Assembly, suggested to Moshe Sharett, the foreign minister, that the persecution of the Iraqi Jews should be used as an argument against allowing the return of 100,000 Arab refugees to Israeli territory. Although Israel had offered to accept the return of the latter, the persecution of the Iraqi Jews showed conclusively the necessity of the ingathering of the Jewish Diaspora in Arab countries—which could not take place should the Arabs be allowed to return. Sharett, however, thought it highly unlikely that this would be an acceptable pretext for going back on the Israeli offer and cautioned against drawing analogies between the

Iraqi Jews and the Arab refugees. Sharett's caution is in great contrast to the eagerness of Iraqi ministers and some U.S. and British diplomats to effect such a linkage.[52]

Nūrī resigned office and 'Alī Jawdat al-Ayyūbī replaced him on 10 December 1949. The new administration was short-lived, resigning on 1 February. By a decree of 17 December, however, 'Alī Jawdat had abolished martial law. Also, the left-leaning minister of justice, Ḥusayn Jamīl, a lawyer who was scandalized by the abuse of power on the part of the military courts, proposed a decree that would remedy some of the flagrant abuses and also pardon their victims and release them from prison.[53] The lifting of martial law immediately led to an increase in the number of Jews illegally leaving the country. In his report for January 1950, the consul general in Basra reported that the continuing flight of Jews from Basra was the topic of the bazaar and the newspapers. With martial law abolished the penalty for being caught was much less serious, and elements of the police and the army were "assisting" the illegal migration: one army officer was caught smuggling Jews in his truck for a bribe of £3,000.

Nor were the reasons for the flight far to seek. As the consul general reported, it was "plain nonsense" to pretend that there was no discrimination. Jews were driven out of every government department and swept out of the port administration. Import licenses were refused to Jewish merchants, and their goods subjected to inordinate delays in customs. Jewish doctors could not have their licenses renewed and thus could not practice. The conditions described by the consul general in Basra also obtained everywhere else in Iraq, as a despatch of 7 March 1950 from the Baghdad embassy made clear. As this despatch furthermore pointed out, there was a constant fear that martial law would be reimposed and "again expose the Jewish community to the injustices which they had suffered during 1948–9."[54]

A few days before this despatch was sent, a bill had been enacted to enable Iraqi Jews to divest themselves of their nationality and leave the country for good. When the bill was debated in the Senate, Ezra Daniel intervened with two speeches, saying that

> he did not know what the Jew could do in Iraq after he had been submitted to the exceptional conditions of the past two years. He had not been admitted to the Higher Colleges and was not allowed to study at his own expense abroad. Work was denied to him and he suffered restrictions in business. But for the severe handicaps, Iraqi Jews would not have gone so far as to attempt large scale flight from the country.

The Iraqi Jews, Senator Daniel declared

> are now deprived of their constitutional and legal rights as a result of administrative measures placing exceptional restrictions on them alone of all Iraqi nationals. They have been discriminated against and their liberties, actions, education and means of livelihood have been handicapped. Does not the Government [he asked] consider it to be its duty to reassure this large section of loyal citizens by removing those extraordinary restrictions in order to restore to Iraqi Jews their sense of security, confidence and stability? The Jews [he went on] have lived in Iraq for 3,500 years. That is why they are reluctant to emigrate unless they are really obliged to do so.[55]

Speaking freely in an official forum, Ezra Daniel was able in these two speeches to set out the position to which Iraqi Jews had been reduced in less than two years. This was the first and the last time that anyone was able to speak for them publicly in their own country.

As has been said, the occasion was a debate over the bill that would allow Iraqi Jews to renounce their nationality and depart without possibility of return. This bill was introduced in Parliament by Tawfīq al-Suwaidī's administration, which followed 'Alī Jawdat's. Suwaidī had assumed office on 5 February. On 25 February he told Humphrey Trevelyan (in charge of the embassy in Mack's absence) that a bill on this subject was being prepared. It is not entirely clear why Suwaidī's administration, soon after coming into office, decided on such a step; the reason he gave was that a growing number of Jews were leaving illegally for Iran—probably thirty or forty a day. Trevelyan reported that the *mutaṣarrif* of Basra had told the consul general that this flow of illegal emigrants was undermining administration in his province "because the bribes available were so heavy and so tempting." Suwaidī estimated that some six or seven thousand would avail themselves of the law. On 2 March the bill was introduced into, and approved by, the Chamber of Deputies; two days later the Senate also voted in favor.[56]

The law, which was to be in force for one year, was silent about the disposition of the property of those who availed themselves of it. When consulted by Suwaidī, Trevelyan advised inter alia that the Iraqi government "should study the action taken by the Israeli Government in respect of the property left behind by the Arab refugees." This was precisely to establish a link between the fate of the Palestinian Arab refugees and the Jews of Iraq. The former had fled and been dispossessed in the course of a war that their own leaders and the

Arab states who had championed their cause had fought and lost; the latter had fought no war and had no part in the events that had taken place in Palestine after 15 May 1948. Trevelyan's advice went far toward accepting the Iraqi thesis that Iraqi Jews had no right to be in Iraq—although the embassy had cautioned the previous September against admitting such a proposition. The Iraqi thesis was indeed aired both in the Chamber of Deputies, where Isma'il al-Ghānim called the Iraqi Jews traitors, and in the Senate, where Muṣṭafa al-'Umarī inquired why the Iraqi government had not frozen Jewish property in the same way that Israel had frozen Arab property. For the time being, the government chose not to follow up Trevelyan's advice or 'Umarī's question, and simply decided that those leaving Iraq under the law would be allowed to take with them the sum of £50. There may have been nothing sinister in this decision: Iraq was suffering from a shortage of foreign currency, and Suwaidī believed anyway that those likely to want to go would be poor.[57] But the threat of expropriation made privately by Nūrī in 1949, and its public advocacy by 'Umaraī and others, the hint by Trevelyan that what befell the Palestinian Arabs might justify something similar in the case of the Iraqi Jews—all these were, as the sequel showed, straws in the wind, signs and omens. But those to be so soon and so disastrously to be affected were, however, quite unaware of what was happening.

The passage of the act allowing renunciation of Iraqi citizenship did not lead immediately to a rush of applications. But it did not serve, either, to ease the position of the Jews or lead to less discrimination. Attacks in nationalist newspapers increased. The Jews were accused of waging a cold war against the Iraqi economy, by paralyzing trade and pretending to be bankrupt in order to rob the people of their money; they were also accused of impoverishing Iraq by smuggling large quantities of cash and valuables. These attacks aroused increasing fear among the Jews, who withdrew more and more from business. Monetary scarcity and economic stagnation followed, and a vicious circle was created in which fear and stagnation of trade fed on one another. The minister of finance, 'Abd al-Karīm al-Uzrī, then called a meeting of Baghdad bank managers to seek advice on dealing with the situation. The manager of the government-owned Rafidain Bank, Muḥammad 'Alī al-Chalabī, was inclined to blame the Jews for making things difficult. Ṭālib Mushtāq, of the Arab Bank was much more virulent, accusing the Jews of deliberately sabotaging the economy of Iraq. The managers of the three British banks—the Eastern Bank, the Imperial Bank of Iran, and the Ottoman Bank—suggested that the minister, to restore confidence, should make a statement "which would assure the Jews that it was not the Government's intention to freeze their assets." Uzri was unwilling to do so, "on the grounds that statements had already been made in Parliament and he did not want to add to them."[58] Uzrī's reluctance is possibly significant, perhaps even sinister.

Suwaidī's law, whatever the motives and expectations of its promoters, made possible the swift dissolution of the community, which, within one year, ceased to exist in any meaningful sense. As has been seen, the Zionist underground consisted of a very small number of mostly young activists, and it had been seriously disrupted by the police in the autumn of 1949. During the year of its currency, however, the new law was to transform this insignificant underground into the secret and unaccountable government of the community. As noted previously, the official head of the community, Ḥakhām Sasōn, resigned at the end of 1949, following attacks upon him and his policy that may quite possibly have been instigated by the Zionist underground. He was succeeded by a notable with influential connections, Ḥesqēl Shemṭōb, who seems to have been more friendly to Zionism than his predecessor. The Suwaidī law was enacted shortly after he took office. The numbers of Jews expected to take advantage of the law was thought to be small. Even so, the official heads of the community seem to have made no effort to ascertain what the fate of the emigrants' property would be; nor did they concern themselves with the conditions and arrangements relating to the emigrants' departure.

Into this vacuum the Zionist underground inserted itself and ended by taking over the functions of the official communal bodies. Soon after the passage of the law, two Zionist emissaries came to Baghdad. One was an English Jewish journalist, Ronald Barnett, who had served in the British forces in the Middle East during the war and had become acquainted with various local political figures, and was working for the Jewish Agency. The other was Shlomo Hillel, who had been born in Baghdad, gone as a child to Palestine, and subsequently joined a kibbutz. In 1946 he had visited Baghdad under an assumed name to establish liaison between the Zionist underground and the Jewish Agency organization in charge of illegal immigration. He subsequently went to Iran under another assumed name in order to facilitate the smuggling of Jews from Iraq to Iran and thence to

Israel. Now at age twenty-seven he came to Baghdad in the guise of a British subject, by name Richard Armstrong. According to Hillel's account, prior to their arrival, he and Barnett had broached a deal in Rome with the managing director of a Baghdad travel agency, Iraq Tours. It was awarded a franchise for the transportaion of the Jews from Iraq, in collaboration with Near East Air Transport, of which Barnett was an executive. The deal, which must have proved very lucrative for Iraq Tours, was clinched when Barnett and Hillel reached Baghdad and met Tawfīq al-Suwaidī, who was a shareholder in Iraq Tours.[59] But Iraq Tours was not allowed to keep all of these profits for itself. Ṣabāḥ al-Sa'īd, son of Nūrī and managing director of Iraqi Airways, objected forcefully to this exclusive arrangement, and he was squared by being allowed a royalty on each body transported by Near East. The deal with Suwaidī, it would seem, took place in the presence of Ḥesqēl Shemṭōb, who was a friend of the prime minister's.[60]

This arrangement was kept secret from the Jews who were its object. Control of the transport arrangements was in the hands of the Zionist underground, with the approval of the government and of the communal authorities. The underground also took control of the official formalities, of registration and the like, that would be required of prospective emigrants. This control, writes Meer Baṣrī, who served at the time as acting head of the community, was under Shemṭōb's "nominal supervision." That the supervision was indeed nominal we may gather from a cryptic reference in Hillel's account to "incursions" on Shemṭōb's "prerogatives during the difficult early months of the airlift."[61] Again, when Baṣrī was acting head during Shemṭōb's absence abroad in the summer of 1950, he found the position awkward and difficult. He writes that he "could not remedy the situation" and asked the minister of the interior to remove the emigration formalities from the supervision of the communal authorities; on Shemṭōb's return, he handed in his resignation.

Baṣrī gives an inkling of some of the abuses arising from the exercise of this secret, uncontrolled, and usurped power on the part of the youthful and generally unknown members of the underground.

> The prospects augured well at first and matters moved on smoothly [writes Baṣrī of the early days of the implementation of Suwaidī's law]. However, after a few weeks I received complaints about travel procedures. People who relinquished their Iraqi nationality and registered for emigration waited for several weeks and even months whereas others, more fortunate, were able to leave the country in a matter of days. Moreover, poor emigrants who had

gold rings or extra luggage [which the Iraqi officials would not allow them to take with them] were asked to leave them with the young man arranging the voyage to carry them safely to Israel (I understand that these valuables deposited in trust were not handed back later to their owners in Israel). Many men who gave their Iraqi money to be transferred to their new abode lost their savings or most of them. I spoke to Mr. Shemtob, but he could do nothing in the matter.[62]

As has been seen, when Suwaidī's law was passed, it was thought that the number of those wishing to leave Iraq for Israel would not exceed ten thousand; and in fact registrations were few at the outset, and very slow to gather momentum. But after the first few months registrations gathered pace very quickly, and when the law expired at the end of March 1951, the vast majority had elected to go to Israel, with only about thirteen thousand choosing to remain Iraqi citizens. That registrations accelerated as time went on resulted to some extent from a snowball effect. As members of a family registered for emigration, others felt compelled to follow suit, and as more were going, more and more felt that they had better do the same. Again, bombs were thrown at places of Jewish resort, which must have increased the fear. It has still not been established who was responsible for these acts. What cannot be controverted is that the emigrants were given no idea of what awaited them in Israel, the communal authorities made no attempt to establish what would befall the emigrants' property, and they did not even caution their charges about the possible financial risks involved in giving up their citizenship. The authorities seem, in fact, to have left the whole affair in the hands of the underground, which either followed its own whims or obeyed directions from Israel. We learn from Hillel that Levi Eshkol, the treasurer of the Jewish Agency, informed him that Israel did not have the ability to absorb the Iraqi Jews in any great numbers; he was to tell them that they must not rush: "We don't even have tents. If they come, they'll have to live in the street." But when Hillel consulted Ben-Gurion, he was told: "You're going to bring Jews. Tell them to come quickly. What if the Iraqis suddenly change their minds and rescind the law? Go and bring them quickly." When the Suwaidī law was passed, the Israeli foreign minister, Moshe Sharett, announced the event to Israeli missions abroad in a circular telegram of 5 March 1950. In it he speculated on the reason that had led to this legislation. One reason, he declared, was that the Iraqi government had probably been tempted by the prospect of "spoliation [of] Jewish property," the fate of which was now "gravely uncertain."[63] About these fears, the Iraqi Jews were kept completely in the dark.

Suwaidī resigned on 12 September 1950 and Nūrī succeeded him. There were then about eighty thousand Jews who had given up their Iraqi nationality, and Nūrī sought to use them both to embarrass Israel and to score a point in Pan-Arab politics. On 23 November, Mack cabled the Foreign Office that Nūrī declared that he could not keep such numbers of stateless Jews in Iraq. He embarked on a "tirade" to the effect that Israel could not plead that she could not receive them, in view of the Zionist insistence on unrestricted immigration during the mandate. About a month later, H. Beeley (who was then a member of the Baghdad embassy) reported to the Eastern Department that Iraqi ministers were saying that "the creation of so many stateless Jews at one time . . . would compel the Government either to drive them across a land frontier (Kuwait is the current favourite) or to intern them in concentration camps." About a month afterward Nūrī attempted to get the Jordanians to agree to allow trucks filled with the stateless Jews to be driven across their territory so that they could be dumped at the borders of Israel. King 'Abdullah and his prime minister, Samīr al-Rifā'ī, refused point blank; Nūrī tried to involve the British ambassador, Sir Alec Kirkbride; and Nūrī and Samīr nearly came to blows in his study. Shortly before, to his credit, 'Abdullah had offered to the Israelis the use of Mafraq airfield to facilitate the passage of the stateless Jews from Iraq to Israel.[64]

Nūrī was not content with these private approaches. His speech at the end of November 1950 to the Constitutional Union Party, of which he was president, was full of demagogy and incitement:

> Should not justice [he asked] take its course and stretch out its hands to punish certain people whom we call "citizens"? These people exploited the wealth of this country, possessed large properties, and came to enjoy prominent commercial standings in this country, but actively assisted the enemies of the country, who fought against us, with financial subsidies supported by official documents.[65]

Nūrī kept his masterstroke until the currency of Suwaidī's law expired, in March 1951. There were then very large numbers of now-stateless Iraqi Jews waiting in Baghdad to be transported to Israel. On 10 March, a secret session of the Chamber of Deputies passed a law freezing all Jewish property and vesting it in a director general of Jewish frozen property. On the very same day, again in a secret session, the Senate ratified the law. Ten days later, another law, also approved on the nod by the Chamber and the Senate, provided for the confiscation of the property of Iraqi Jews who were then abroad and who did not return within two months. Under both laws, Jews who had not applied to leave under Suwaidī's law, or those who had been ordinarily resident abroad, had to prove this to the authorities before they could regain control of their property.[66] The second law dealt with Iraqi citizens who had not expressed any intention of giving up their citizenship; it thus discriminated against a group of Iraqis and was, on the face of it, unconstitutional.

This legislation aroused immediate protest on the part of the Board of Deputies of British Jews, and of various members of Parliament, on the score that it violated the declaration signed by Iraq on its admission to the League of Nations in 1932 in which it bound itself to provide just and equal treatment to all its nationals regardless of racial, religious, or linguistic differences. These guarantees, according to the declaration, were "obligations of international concern" and "placed under the guarantee of the League of Nations." Any member of the League Council who considered that Iraq was not abiding by the declaration had the right to refer the matter to the Permanent Court of International Justice for adjudication and decision. In a paper dated 25 April 1951, Lionel Heald, K.C., M.P. argued that the guarantees and safeguards provided by the declaration were intended to be permanent, "since it was only upon the basis of their observance that the League agreed to the determination of the Mandate" whereby Britain had been charged with the government of Iraq. Furthermore, it was Britain that had sponsored Iraq's admission to the League. Heald thus concluded by arguing that it was the duty of the British government "as the former Mandatory Power and a party to the treaty or convention of 1932, to insist upon the cancellation of [these discriminatory laws] and if necessary to secure the reference to the International Court of Justice of the alleged breach by Iraq of her solemn international obligations."[67]

In a long opinion of 18 May 1951, which reviewed the legal position in the light of the South-West Africa case considered by the International Court of Justice and which involved undertakings given (by South Africa) to the League, G. H. Fitzmaurice concluded that "there really is a lot to be said for the view put forward by Mr. Heald and his friends." But, he argued, the fact

> that we may have a bare legal right to take Iraq to the Court if we like to start a dispute with her about whether she is observing the Declaration does not, of course, mean that we are in any way obliged to do this.

The declaration had been made a long time ago, and

> we cannot admit that after the passage of nearly twenty years, during which Iraq has been a fully independent State and entered the United Nations as an original member, H.M. Government still retain some special moral obligation in the matter.[68]

Refusal to assume responsibility for actions of the Iraqi government that contravened undertakings given by it and, in effect, underwritten by Britain was nothing new. This had been the stance adopted following the termination of the Mandate. On that occasion Lord Hailsham, the lord chancellor, stood in the House of Lords to affirm with brilliant forensic argumentation that when the British representative had declared in the Permanent Mandate Commission that if Iraq should prove unworthy of the confidence placed in her, "the moral responsibility must rest with His Majesty's Government," he "was not saying and never was saying, and was never understood to say, that he was guaranteeing in the future, that His Majesty's Government would protect minorities in Iraq, and would assume a moral responsibility with regard to them."[69]

It stood to reason that responsibility disclaimed in 1933 was not going to be acknowledged in 1951. Furthermore there was now a new element that made it even less necessary to acknowledge any obligation. When the law freezing the emigrants' property was passed, the Israeli foreign minister stated in the Knesset that "by freezing the property of tens of thousands of Jewish immigrants to Israel . . . the Government of Iraq has opened a reckoning between itself and the State of Israel." Sharrett here opened the door to linking the fate of the Iraqi Jews to that of the Palestinian Arab refugees—precisely what he had deprecated two years earlier. This line of thought was to be considerably developed in the Foreign Office. On Sharett's statement an official, P. A. Rhodes, minuted: "I am glad Mr. S. has agreed that the two accounts should be linked."[70] In setting out the possible terms of a reply to Lionel Heald, Fitzmaurice suggested that he might be told that it was up to any country that considered that Iraq was treating part of its population in a manner inconsistent with the Charter to bring the matter before the United Nations.[71] Briefing Kenneth Younger, the minister of state, who was to answer a question from a Labor M.P., Gordon Lang, whether the government would take steps to urge Iraq to withdraw laws that violated their undertaking of 1932, another official, J.C. Wardrop, admitted that the laws were inconsistent with the obligations Iraq had assumed toward the League. But he argued that "there were insufficient grounds for a formal approach to the Iraqi Government, the more so," he added, "since the Israelis themselves had laid themselves open to the charge of discrimination against their own Arab minority."[72] A later Foreign Office comment develops in all its fullness the line adumbrated in the minutes just quoted. Iraqi actions against Iraqi Jews, it was declared, "reflect the feelings aroused throughout the Arab world by the sufferings of the Palestine Arabs."[73] Arab refugees, in their hundred thousands have lost their homes. They have little or no prospect of seeing them again, or receiving compensation for their property or the bank balances frozen by Israel: in this political arithmetic, the two accounts, of the Iraqi Jews, and of the Arab refugees, fortunately, stand in perfect symmetry and precise balance.

The Iraqi legislation, which made stateless individuals of Iraqi Jews living abroad, created a vexing problem for the British government. There were about twenty-five of these cases in Britain. What to do about them? Papers and minutes went back and forth between the Home Office and the Foreign Office. Should they be sent back to Iraq? But they were no longer citizens of Iraq. Should they be sent to Israel? But how could this be done against their will? The problem of the twenty-five, in the end, had to be put to the two secretaries of state. The relevant Foreign Office file carries an annotation by the foreign secretary:

> Much better [wrote Anthony Eden] if those Jews could go to Palestine. We cannot force them to go there, but should we not encourage them?
> Poor England.[74]

The foreign secretary could not perhaps have known of the complicated chain of events that, from General Maude's entry into Baghdad to Cornwallis's prohibition of such an entry and beyond, had led to the disagreeable problem of the twenty-five landing on his desk. The expression of self-pity with which the minute ends does seem, all the same, excessive. That he should have given expression to it speaks volumes about his character as about his judgment. For what threatened, and finally subverted, the British position in the Middle East was infinitely more formidable than anything that the hapless twenty-five could do. Poor England indeed.

NOTES

1. See Elie Kedourie, *The Chatham House Version* (London, 1970), p. 437 fn. 65, for the figures at the end of the First World War.

2. Quoted in Elie Kedourie, *Arabic Political Memoirs and Other Studies* (London, 1974), p. 142.

3. Wingate Papers, School of Oriental Studies, Durham University, 150/5. There is no indication to whom the paper, entitled "The Political Future of Iraq," was addressed; but at the bottom of the memorandum it is noted that two copies were to go to Colonel [Stewart] Symes, Sir Reginald Wingate's private secretary at the Cairo Residency in 1917–19, hence presumably its presence among Wingate's papers.

4. See Elie Kedourie, *England and the Middle East* (London, 1956), chap. 7; idem, *The Chatham House Version*, chaps. 9, 10; idem, "The Iraqi Shi'is and their Fate," *Shi'ism, Resistance and Revolution,* ed. Martin Kramer (London, 1987).

5. Fayṣal's memorandum, dated March 1933, is reproduced in 'Abd al-Razzāq al-Ḥasanī, *Tarīkh al-wizārāt al-irāqiyya* (History of Iraqi Cabinets), 4th ed. (Beirut, 1974), vol. 3, pp. 323–30.

6. Kedourie, *The Chatham House Version*, p. 273; Ṭālib Mushtāq, *Awrāq Ayyāmī* (Records of My Days) (Beirut, 1968), vol. 1, p. 203.

7. Mushtāq, *Awrāq Ayyāmī*, vol. 1, pp. 189–92.

8. The Club, declared Jamālī in 1958, was "a nationalist school for the young"; evidence at his trial before the Special Military Court, Baghdad, following the coup d'état of 14 July 1958, *Proceedings* (in Arabic) (Baghdad, 1959), vol. 3, p. 1089.

9. Ḥasanī, *Tarīkh*, vol. 5, p. 208; and Qāwuqji, *Mudhakkirāt* (Memoirs) (Beirut, 1975), vol. 2, pp. 10–17.

10. Anwar Sha'ūl, *Qiṣṣat ḥayātī fī wādī al-rāfidayn* (The Story of My Life in Mesopotamia) (Jerusalem, 1980), pp. 213-14; Abraham Ḥayyim Twena, *Golim u-Geulin* (The Exiled and the Redeemed), (Ramla, 1977), vol. 6, pp. 17—18.

11. Sha'ūl, *Qiṣṣat ḥayātī fi wādī al-rāfidayn*, pp. 214–15; Akram Zu'aytar, *Yawmiyyāt . . . 1935–1939* (Diaries . . . 1935–1939) (Beirut, 1980), pp. 418–19 and 426, entries for 29 July and 10 August 1938. The entries in these

diaries show that these events took place not under Hāshimī's administration but about two years later.

12. Zu'aytar, *Yawmiyyāt*, p. 597.

13. Ibid., p. 369.

14. Ibid., pp. 476–85, which quotes and summarizes the deliberations of the Congress.

15. Ibid., pp. 588, 591–92, 607–8.

16. Elie Kedourie, "The Sack of Basra and the *Farhud* in Baghdad," in *Arabic Political Memoirs and Other Studies*, pp. 283–91.

17. "British officers later told me," wrote Archie Roosevelt, who in 1944–45 served in the U.S. legation in Baghdad, "[that] they could hear the screams of Jewish women in the night as they waited on the West Bank of the Tigris for dawn to break" *(For Lust of Knowing: Memoirs of an Intelligence Officer* [London, 1988], p. 136). What these officers were waiting for is not explained, since they were not permitted to cross to the east bank so long as the disorders lasted.

18. Kedourie, "Sack of Basra," pp. 291–309. A testimony from the horse's mouth is useful confirmation. While on an anti-Zionist propaganda tour in the United States, (Dame) Freya Stark was asked at a meeting in Boston whether the British Army had marched into Baghdad and wrecked it in 1941. As she wrote in a letter of 30 May 1944 to Elizabeth Monroe, her colleague in the Ministry of Information, she was able in reply "to give an eyewitness account of how the British troops were kept outside and never entered the town at all while the Iraqis dealt with their own little massacres in their own way"; Freya Stark, *Letters* ((Salisbury, England, 1978), vol. 4, pp. 99–100. Dame Freya Stark's jocular and lighthearted reference to the Iraqis' "little massacres" strikes exactly the right tone.

19. F.O. 624/38/502, report by R. Catling, Assistant Inspector General 'C', C.I.D., Palestine Police, on visit to Iraq 6–22 January 1944. The report is dated 24 January.

20. E. M. H. Lloyd, *Food and Inflation in the Middle East, 1940–45* (Stanford, 1956), pp. 237–38.

21. In a letter to Sir Horace Seymour at the Foreign Office, 25 September 1941, quoted in Kedourie, "Sack of Basra," p. 308.

22. F.O. 371/40090, E 2576/93, Cornwallis's despatch, 15 April 1944, enclosing Wilkins's letter of 8 April previous. Hankey's minute is of 2 May.

23. Stark, *Letters*, vol. 4, p. 223.

24. Mushtāq, *Awrāq Ayyāmī*, pp. 479, 498.

25. A great deal has been published about the Zionist underground in Iraq. See, most recently, Shlomo Hillel, *Operation Babylon* (London, 1987). The author went in disguise to Baghdad from Palestine/Israel, in 1946 and in 1950, in order to organize Jewish emigration.

26. F.O.. 371/68446, E 2356/27/93, minute by J. C. B. Richmond enclosed with letter from G. C. Pelham, Baghdad, to B. A. B. Burrows, Eastern Depart-

ment, 24 January 1948. The embassy had itself independently heard of these rumors; ibid., E 2217, G. C. Pelham's despatch, 25 January.

27. F.O. 624/127, minute of 7 May 1948, initialed H. B. M[ack].

28. Hasanī, *Tarikh*, vol. 8, pp. 17–18.

29. F.O. 371/68459, E 9674/111/93.

30. F.O. 371/68450, E 9745/27/93.

31. F.O. 371/68459, E 13515/111/93.

32. F.O. 371/68451, E 11708/27/93, letter from Richmond to Burrows, 1 September 1948.

33. F.O. 371/68459, E 1270/111/93.

34. F.O. 371/68451, E 12058/27/93, Mack's telegram, Baghdad, 16 September 1948, and Clinton-Thomas's minute, 17 September.

35. F.O. 371/68451, E 12321/27/93, Mack's telegram, Baghdad 21 September 1948; F.O. 371/68452, E 12930/27/93, Mack's letter, 24 September 1948, to Michael Wright, Eastern Department. On the Regent's behavior in 1941, see Kedourie, "Sack of Basra, pp. 298–300.

36. F.O. 371/68452, E 12443/27/93, telegram from Mack, Baghdad, 24 September 1948; and Mack's letter to Wright of the same date in E 12930 cited in note 35, and Walker's minute of 6 October on this letter.

37. Ḥasanī, *Tarīkh*, vol. 8, pp. 17–23.

38. F.O. 624/165, Richmond's minute, 3 February 1949.

39. F.O. 624/165.

40. Hillel, *Operation Babylon*, pp. 214–23. As regards Ḥakhām Sasōn's character and policy, see Emile Marmorstein's article originally published in December 1949, and reproduced as "Hakham Sason in 1949," *Middle Eastern Studies* (July, 1988).

41. Copy of al-Kabīr's evidence in F.O. 371/52514, E 3213/4/31.

42. F.O. 371/75336, E 1008/1016/31, Mack's telegram, Baghdad, 20 January 1949; F.O. 371/75182, E 2539/1571/93, Mack's telegram, Baghdad, 24 February 1949.

43. F.O.. 624/150; only the first sheet of this minute has survived, the rest being subsequently destroyed by official action.

44. *Documents on the Foreign Policy of Israel*, vol. 2, *October 1948–1949* (Jerusalem, 1984), no. 526, Eytan, Lausanne, 30 April 1949 to Sharett. For McGhee's endeavors over the Palestinian refugee problem, see his *Envoy to the Middle World* (New York, 1983), chap. 4 passim.

45. I am grateful to Mr. Shabtai Teveth, Ben-Gurion's biographer, for the relevant extract from Ben-Gurion's diary.

46. *Documents on the Foreign Policy of Israel*, vol. 4, *May–December 1949* (Jerusalem, 1986), no. 350, Eban to Sharett, New York, 18 October 1949; no. 357, Elath to Sharett, Washington, 19 October 1949.

47. F.O. 371/75158, E 9354/113/93, Chadwick's minute, 23 July 1949.

48. F.O. 371/75434, E 9186/1821/31, Mack's telegram, Baghdad, 27 July 1949.

49. F.O. 371/75444, E 12637/1821/31, tel. from Morton (through Houston-Boswall, the British Minister), Beirut, 18 October 1949; F.O. 371/75446, E 13568/1821/31, Chancery, Baghdad to Middle East Secretariat (the Department in the Foreign Office concerned with Palestinian refugee problems), 28 October 1949.

50. F.O. 371/75445, E 13152/1821/31, despatch from Mack, Baghdad. 21 October 1949; F.O. 371/75446, E 13568/1821/31, cited in note 49.

51. F.O. 371/75152, E 9114/1105/93, Middle East Secretariat to Chancery, British Middle East Office, 5 September 1949; E 11795/1105, Chancery B.M.E.O. to M.E. Secretariat, 22 September; E 12290/1105, Chancery Baghdad to M.E. Secretariat, 29 September. This exchange may have given McNeil the idea of a transfer of population, which, as mentioned previously, he broached to Eban shortly afterward.

52. *Documents on the Foreign Policy of Israel*, vol. 4, no. 369, Katznelson to Sharett, New York, 26 October 1949; vol. 4, no. 387, Sharett to Katznelson, Tel Aviv, 4 November 1949.

53. Ḥasanī, *Tarīkh*, vol. 8, pp. 150–51.

54. F.O. 371/82404, EQ 1013/2, Basra monthly report for January 1950; F.O. 371/82478, EQ 1571/8, despatch from Humphrey Trevelyan, acting ambassador, 7 March 1950.

55. F.O. 371/82478, EQ 1571/10, Mack's despatch, Baghdad, 21 March 1950.

56. F.O. 371/82478, EQ 1571/8, cited in note 54; Ḥasanī, *Tarīkh*, vol. 8, pp. 174–75.

57. EQ 1571/8 and 10 (see nn. 54, 55); Ḥasanī, *Tarīkh*, vol. 8, p. 175.

58. F.O. 371/82422, EQ 1103/1, Mack's despatch, Baghdad, 23 March 1950; F.O. 371/82478, EQ 1571/10, in note 55.

59. In his annual review for 1951, the British ambassador, Sir John Troutbeck, remarked that Suwaidī and Muṣṭafa al-'Umarī were both "notorious for their venality." F.O. 371/98733, EQ 1011/1.

60. Details in Hillel, *Operation Babylon*, chap. 11.

61. Ibid., p. 295.

62. Meer S. Baṣrī, "My Part in the Operation," *The Scribe* (June 1988), 5–6.

63. Hillel, *Operation Babylon*, pp. 229–31; *Documents on the Foreign Policy of Israel* (Jerusalem, 1988), vol. 5, p. 175, no. 128.

64. F.O. 371/82486, EQ 1571/52, telegram from Mack, Baghdad, 23 November 1950; and EQ 1571/59, Beeley's letter of 20 December; F. O. 371/91689, EQ 1571/2, Kirkbride's letter to Geoffrey Furlonge at the Foreign Office, 16 January 1951. The incident is recounted in Kirkbride's memoirs, *From the Wings* (London, 1976), pp. 115–16; 'Abdullah's offer was reported by the director general of the Foreign Ministry, Walter Eytan, to Sharett, on

7 November 1950; *Documents on the Foreign Policy of Israel*, vol. 5, no. 448n, translated in *Companion Volume*, p. 232.

65. F.O. 378/82408, EQ 1016/33, translation of Nūrī's speech enclosed with Mack's despatch, Baghdad, 30 November 1950.

66. Text of laws and regulations issued pursuant to them in *The Baghdad Chamber of Commerce Journal* (in Arabic) (Baghdad, 1951), nos. 3–4, 5–6.

67. F.O. 371/91691, EQ 1571/63.

68. F.O. 371/91692, EQ 1571/74.

69. House of Lords Debates, 28 November 1933.

70. F.O. 371/91691, EQ 1571/56, Sharett's statement of 19 March and Rhodes's minute of 2 May.

71. F.O. 371/91691, EQ 1571/74.

72. F.O. 371/91691, EQ 1571/61, Wardrop's minute, 20 April 1951.

73. F.O. 371/91692. EQ 1571/86.

74. F.O. 371/98767, EQ 1571/27, Eden's minute, 7 October 1952.

Religious Orthodoxy or Local Tradition:
Marriage Celebration in Southern Tunisia*

Lucette Valensi

THE SOCIAL practices of the Jewish communities of the Diaspora are generally studied with reference to two frameworks, that of religious and legal orthodoxy on the one hand, and that of the culture of the dominant society on the other. Scholars often tend to analyze these relations in two successive sequences. First they measure to what extent a given community conforms to the general prescriptions of Judaism. Next, whatever appears to be a deviation from, or an adjustment of the norm, they attribute to the surrounding culture. The Jewish practices of any given place are thus conceived as the sum of regular prescriptions plus the borrowings from the majority culture. This approach has the advantage of illuminating the complementary aspects of the phenomena being studied. However, this somewhat arithmetical vision of social practices has two weaknesses. First, it does not seem to take into account the fact that one of the two terms of the equation is variable, namely, the dominant culture. This too has local roots and its own history; it is continually being formed and modified. The second weakness flows from the exaggerated importance assigned to the letter of the law and its exegesis as if the normative discourse represented authenticity and purity while the surrounding environment was a source of contamination and adulteration. Could we conceive of some ethnologist or historian originating in distant parts coming to study our own social practices primarily in relation to the constitution or to our legal codes? This approximates the optical illusion that operates when we study Muslim societies in general, or the minorities of the Muslim world in particular.

---

*This essay was translated from the French by Michael Bonner.

I suggest instead that any culture, even a traditional and traditionalist one, is an ongoing construction; and that the culture of religious or ethnic communities is elaborated in and through interaction between the different components of the social fabric.[1] In this paper, I do not claim to be offering a demonstration of these propositions. I wish only to present a case study that will attempt to avoid the pitfalls just mentioned. I shall describe and compare the wedding festivities of two communities in southern Tunisia, those of the Jews of the island of Jerba and those of the Muslims of Nefta, a town in Jerid.[2] At the same time my reading of these rituals follows the female protagonists of the celebration. In this regard, a brief digression and word of explanation is necessary.

For a number of years I collected the life stories of Jews born around the Mediterranean from the turn of the century through the 1930s.[3] In the course of this work, I was struck by the recurrence of certain patterns in the narratives of North African women. To begin with, these women related the story of their marriage with a profusion of detail. And this was not only, or not always, cast as a romance or a love story, but much more often as a rite of passage. Indeed, it was the only rite of passage that they themselves ever experienced, since for girls neither birth nor puberty is marked by any ritual at all. Accounts of their involvement in other rituals, such as the birth, circumcision, and bar mitzvah of their sons, were distinctly less important and expansive than their descriptions of their own marriages.

Furthermore, the episode was depicted as a moment of keen tension between tradition and practice. By tradition we mean here, in the broad sense, a set of shared rules and values that endure and that are transmitted from generation to generation.[4] Marriage presented the protagonists with an occasion to measure themselves against tradition. The stories emphasized whether the event had completely conformed to tradition or whether some of its usual constraints had been rejected—deliberately or otherwise.

The stories narrated by these women also indicated that, already from childhood, they had been prepared for marriage as for the most important event of their existence. They grew up with the fear that it might not take place—either because no candidate would step forward to ask for their hand or because the parents would be unable to pay the required dowry. As children, they had learned that marriage constitutes an individual and family crisis. As women, they recollected their own trials in great detail.[5] Finally, one last recurring trait of the narratives of North African marriages was that the narrators themselves emphasized that this or that episode represented the truly Jewish canonical sequence of the ritual as a whole. However, what they designated as authentically Jewish did not necessarily correspond to the actual requirements of Jewish marriage law. In fact, five conditions are legally required in order for a marriage to be valid: (1) mutual consent; (2) the absence of legal obstacles; (3) the giving of the *kiddushin* (that is, the groom gives to the bride a ring or any other object of gold or silver, the weight of which is equal to at least half a grain of barley. While giving this piece of precious metal, the man pronounces the formula: "You are now betrothed to me [*mequddeshet*] with this ring." This gift is made publicly before witnesses and has to be accepted); (4) the *ketubbah*, a written contract in which the amount of the dowry and other financial details are indicated; and (5) the blessing of the couple in front of witnesses. Obviously, some of these legal requirements are realized through some ceremonial and exchanges of words, objects, and symbols. Yet these do not appear in the narratives, or at any rate they are not emphasized.

My hypothesis in the following pages is that the aspects of the marriage celebration considered most fundamental by the participants actually derive from local custom—from a vernacular tradition broadly shared by Jews and Muslims. Within this vernacular tradition, the place of religious orthodoxy is, in the end, limited and reduced for both Muslims and Jews. If we insist on searching for a literal application of legal prescriptions in the marriage practice, we lose much of the richness of the experience as it is lived and of the memory that lingers long afterward.[6]

Semiology of the Ritual

A marriage celebration—indeed any ceremony—can be read as a narrative, or better, as the performance of play. Like a play it presents a beginning and an end, with a number of intervening sequences that unfold over a certain interval of time. While the uniting of two individuals remains its central subject, the action exposes several other levels of meaning, since individual aspirations and private choice are intertwined with issues involving the spouses' families and the larger community as well. The stakes here affect an entire set of social relations and transcend the destiny of the two single individuals. Finally, the marriage celebration has its own actors and audience. From the narrative point of view, as soon as the beginning of the action is known, that is, the engagement, the outcome can be anticlimactic. Nonetheless, the performance must take place.

In the case of southern Tunisia, one can speak rather of two parallel performances: the male and female protagonists operate separately from one another. Each is accompanied by individuals of the same gender, either family or peers. These individuals, by their presence, give the action its public character; they also participate actively, playing a variety of roles and thus contributing to the completeness of the ceremony. At the same time, there are constant exchanges of words, objects, food, and symbols between the bridegroom's side and that of the bride. These exchanges, of course, have both a practical and a functional meaning: once you have brought the guests together, you must feed and amuse them. It is also necessary to provide supplies for the new household. To this can be added a symbolic dimension. The distribution of sweets or perfumes, the auspicious words, and the ululation of the women all place the event under the sign of joy. Some of the material objects that are exchanged (a necklace and rings) embody the bond created by the marriage. Other gifts and countergifts reinforce the reciprocal obligations to which the spouses have committed themselves. These exchanges also offer a means for testing the initial harmony between the two families that have allied themselves, of putting their respective qualities face to face, and of obtaining information on the spouses and their households. It is only at the conclusion of this contest that the protagonists advance from potential associates to full partners. Thus, that which was potential at the beginning of the action becomes actualized during the performance and fully realized at its conclusion.[7] But in the end, this is an asymmetrical exchange, since the outcome is that the bridegroom's family gains a woman, whereas the bride's family receives no counterpart.

Here we must underline the fundamental contrast between the preparation and celebration of marriage in the United Sates and what we are describing for North Africa. On the surface, marriage performs the same basic social and demographic functions everywhere: the establishment of a new family unit, as one generation replaces another. But the stakes vary with the time and place, and the modalities of marriage show infinite variety. In the United Sates today, the order of events and the appearance of the actors would be as follows: two individuals, F and M, meet one another. *They* decide to get married. *They* prepare their own wedding together. A ceremony and a reception bring together the spouses, their parents, relatives, friends, and acquaintances. Finally, when the ceremony is over, M and F begin or take up again their life in common. In the North African case study, M and F do not meet; nor do they decide upon their own union, since it is up to their parents to undertake the negotiations. Similarly, it is up to the parents to prepare the celebration, which unfolds in separate performances for the man and the woman. The individuals who are present are not mere guests: they provide a guarantee for the marriage and assure that the whole series of actions will be in conformity with the group's tradition. The spouses are not brought together until the very last phase of the celebration. And finally, they do not immediately form a new unit as a family and household.

From Betrothal to Marriage: Ethnographic Description

The first performance we shall attend takes place in Nefta. It begins with the betrothal of Rabi'a to a young man. Like Rabi'a, he is a Muslim born in Nefta, although he now lives in Tunis. The betrothal could be analyzed on its own as an autonomous episode, since it has its own ritual and is separated from the wedding by a certain interval. But insofar as it lacks its own denouement and constitutes a preliminary to the wedding, we will retain this episode as the initial sequence of the marriage. It is designated as the *khutba*. The young man's mother pays a discreet visit to Rabi'a's mother. The proposal of marriage is made, but she does not expect an immediate answer. On a subsequent occasion, the young man's mother revisits Rabi'a's household and this time receives a positive response. A week or two later, the actual *khutba* takes place. The young man's mother, accompanied by girls, female neighbors, and relatives, brings baskets to Rabi'a's house. These contain the first presents made to the fiancée: textiles, lingerie, kerchiefs, perfumes, henna, and finally a ring. This public ceremony binds the two parties, with the ring the symbol of this commitment. The groom is absent from the preliminaries, as he is from the public *khutba*.

Now let us move to Jerba, to a Jewish family in Hara Kebira, one of the two communities on the island where Khumsana's betrothal is being celebrated. The preliminary arrangements have been made by the women of the groom's entourage—his mother and sisters. Once the offer has been accepted, the public ceremony can take place. This time it is called *ta'līq* (hanging, embracing). Female neighbors and young women flock into the courtyard of the groom's house. His mother wraps herself in her veil and begins the procession that will bring them from his house to Khumsana's; the women and girls who accompany the groom's mother take turns carrying baskets filled with the same presents as those described above, with the exception that the ring is here replaced by a necklace. Khumsana awaits them in the courtyard of her house, surrounded by her sisters and by other women of her family. The groom's mother presents her with the necklace, which she herself fixes on the fiancée's neck (hence the name of this ceremony). Fruits and drink are distributed to all those present. The sweets contained in the baskets are divided into small portions that are then sent to all the families with whom the fiancée's family has close relations. As in the Muslim case, while (female) neighbors and relatives play an active role in all these exchanges, the fiancé remains absent.

Is there anything that makes the first ceremony Muslim and the second one Jewish? All the persons taking part in the first are Muslim, all those in the second are Jewish. Each public ceremony has a different name. But we may observe the same actresses, identical sexual segregation, the same exchanges of words, of gestures, and of objects in both cases. Numerous variants have been observed in southern Tunisia. For example, in areas where people claim to follow Bedouin, as opposed to urban, values, it is often the father of the bridegroom-to-be who initiates the negotiation with the girl's father. Above all, today the suitor himself will most likely indicate his preference to his parents. But the fact remains that the fiancé's family initiates the negotiations and that the two main protagonists passively accept the outcome of these negotiations. They neither see one another nor engage in any direct exchange.

The betrothal is followed by a period that can vary in length from a few months to a year or two. In Rabi'a's case, relations between the two families are minimal during this intermediate phase. When religious holidays occur, the fiancé sends a few small gifts—kerchiefs, henna, small quantities of sweets, pieces of raw meat. Among the Jews of Jerba, in addition to the presents that the women of the fiancé's household bring to that of the fiancée on the occasion of religious holidays (sweets, jewels, fabric), there are weekly exchanges of cooked dishes. On Friday evening the fiancé's family sends a plate of couscous to the family with which it has become allied; the latter returns the dish laden with a couscous that it has prepared. At this stage the greatest difference between the practice of the Muslims and that of the Jews is that the regulated exchanges that punctuate the period extending from the betrothal to the wedding, and that reiterate the engagement concluded between the two families, follow the rhythms of the religious calendar. They mark the great holidays and, for the Jews, the celebration of the Sabbath. The religious calendar will remain a factor in the subsequent phase. Indeed, the marriage must fit into one of the sequences of the year when celebrations are allowed; within that sequence the days propitious for the celebration are determined. These dates differ for the two religious communities.

Rabi'a's wedding unfolds over three days, corresponding to three distinct sequences, each of which bears a name: the *'utriya*, the *kiswa*, and the *dukhla*. On the day of the *'utriya*, while exchanges between Rabi'a's and the bridegroom's households occur on an intensified level, it is in the former that the action takes place, with Rabi'a in the starring role. At this stage the fiancé's participation is at its low point.

This classic rite of passage shows several phases of separation.[8] On the morning of the *'utriya*, Rabi'a ends a period of seclusion that has lasted for three days, during which she has avoided seeing her father and her brothers, in other words, the male members of the household. Now comes a new separation: very early in the morning, Rabi'a, accompanied by girls of her own age, visits the marabouts. They bring candles and incense, and spend some time near the tombs. Later in the morning, the women of the bridegroom's household bring the *'utriya*, that is, two sewn baskets, containing the objects that are going to be used later in the afternoon: henna, jewels, and slippers for the bride. The latter is now seated in the middle of a room covered by a white silk fabric, surrounded by unmarried girls who will take care of her throughout the entire marriage, and who will do the cooking and cleaning. A female relative of the bridegroom presents her with the *'utriya*.

Thereupon the henna, which has been prepared and then divided into small portions, is sent by the bride's mother to the neighboring houses. This serves as an invitation to the feast, which will take place in the afternoon. While the baskets of the *'utriya* are being transported, the *karrīta* (literally cart, today replaced by a pickup truck [*camionette*]) also travels from the husband's to the wife's house. It is loaded with drinks, vegetables, couscous, and an animal, all of which is to be prepared in the bride's house and later served during the feast. The bride's household makes its first countergift to the bridegroom's by sending back the part of the trousseau that they are expected to provide, that is, the kitchen equipment and a china closet in which all of the kitchenware will be exhibited.

During the afternoon, a new ritual of separation takes place for the girl. She goes to the bath—*hammām*—accompanied by the same girls who went with her to visit the marabouts. It is the groom who must pay for this bath. At the very same time, the bridegroom's father and brothers go to the bride's house, where the ceremony of the *'aqd* takes place. A scribe, *'ādil,* draws up the marriage contract, or *sdaq,* before the father and brothers of the two spouses, together with other witnesses. This contract begins with a Koranic invocation, then identifies the two parties and the obligations that they are undertaking, particularly with respect to their parents. While the contract is being drawn up, the bride's family distributes drinks and cakes to those who are watching the ceremony.

Late in the afternoon the public part of the celebrations begins. Rabi'a is exhibited, festooned with jewels. The women of those households that have received the announcement of the event (in the form of the packets of henna) now flock together in their holiday best, also festooned with jewels. Musicians play while the women dance. A couscous is served to all those present. Meanwhile, in the husband's house a private ceremony takes place, without any guests from outside the family, and without any professional musicians. But people sing and dance, without joining the festivities in the other house. Late in the evening the last sequence of this first day takes place. Rabi'a dons a full pink dress, a black headdress, and an abundance of jewels. A woman applies henna to her hands and feet. Finally, a second countergift is sent to the bridegroom's house, this time to the bridegroom himself: the bride has a bit of henna enclosed in a new handkerchief sent to him. This henna is applied to the palm of the fiancé's hand.

The second day, the day of the *kiswa,* is also called the man's marriage, *'ars er-rajl.* It is indeed his family, if not the bridegroom himself, that now plays the leading role. A main ceremony consists of a procession in the early afternoon. A marching band accompanies the bridegroom's family, and the men carry rifles with which they fire salvos during the procession. A group of men followed by a group of women march behind the musicians. The object of this procession is to transport the *kiswa,* the wardrobe (toilette) contained in two suitcases. The bridegroom's mother, unveiled on this day, also brings a large dish of semolina and a piece of meat to Rabi'a's house. Once it has arrived at the threshold, the procession comes to a halt. The musicians enter first, followed by the groom's family and close friends. The *kiswa* is set down and singing and dancing begin. The public celebration, however, does not occur here in the bride's house. Rather the women gather in the groom's house, and the male relatives retire from the scene. In the courtyard the women form a circle, a professional band plays, and the bridegroom's mother and sisters begin the dancing, soon joined by the other women. A couscous is served to those present—and brought to the husbands who have been sent off to their own quarters.

In Rabi'a's house the *kiswa* is exhibited piece by piece. Once again the women of the family make merry, in a close circle. In the evening henna is again applied to Rabi'a's arms and legs.

The third day, the *dukhla*, is also called the woman's marriage, *'ars el–mra*. In the morning Rabi'a undergoes a general depilation. A sugar-based paste has now replaced both the clay, which was formerly used as a depilatory agent for the body, and the fava bean powder mixed with egg, which was used for the face. The women gather to sing and dance. The groom, for his part, goes to the *hammām* with his male peers. In the afternoon the young woman is arrayed in a two-colored silk dress, embroidered with golden threads. She is then exhibited in the courtyard, perched on a mattress that has been placed on a table. Hiding her face in her hands, she walks in a circle seven times on the mattress. Then she puts on a colored silk veil and remains on view in this array. Once evening has fallen, the groom's family comes for her in a car and sets her down, covered, before her bridegroom's house. She breaks an egg and puts a little henna on a doorpost at the entry. Then she enters the house and remains sitting on a bed in the bridal chamber. The groom's family offers a meal to Rabi'a's family. On both sides, only the members of the family take part in this ceremony, to the exclusion of the neighbors and the other guests. The groom is absent, or at any rate he has remained secluded since the beginning of the day. After going to the *hammām*, he has celebrated with his friends in a house that has been reserved for him, and then, in the afternoon he has gone to the barber. In the evening, his court of young males dress him in his room, in the presence of musicians who sing religious chants. He shares a couscous with his peers, before being led once again to the house that has been reserved for him.

The young men sing and dance, and no women are present. Next, the groom goes on foot with several friends to visit some marabouts and then to the mosque, where the *fātiha* is read.

Toward midnight, the groom finally returns home. This reentry constitutes the *dukhla*: carrying some sweets that are supposed to sweeten the effects of defloration he enters the room where Rabi'a has been waiting. The door closes. The men of his party wait close by for the garment stained with blood to be exhibited. When this is produced, the women ululate, and the men fire a few volleys. The groom then goes out of his room and leaves in the company of his friends.

Various rituals intended to integrate the couple back into normal life continue until the seventh day after the wedding, accompanied by frequent exchanges between the families of the spouses.

In the case of the Jerban Jews, the wedding cycle lasts for ten days. The curtain rises on the bride's house on a Monday night, and the action culminates on the Thursday evening of the following week in her bridegroom's domicile. Because of the temporal extension of Jewish ceremonial, it does not coincide exactly with the ritual we have just followed in Nefta. Instead, we observe various transformations of these rituals. Sometimes the gestures unfold over a longer time, as if the scene were being played in slow motion, or else the sequences are subdivided into distinct episodes. Sometimes the rituals are repeated. Other times they are played out on different scales, as with the episodes of the little and the great hennas, as we shall see later. Other differences between the practices of the Jerid and those of the Jews of Jerba do not derive simply from differences in duration. We shall now describe and analyze them.

The Jewish women of Jerba are night owls.[9] Besides, in the Jewish tradition the day begins at night. Celebrations therefore usually begin at nightfall. The first one begins on Monday evening, a procession of the women and girls of the bridegroom's household carry baskets containing sweets, dried fruits, and gum to the fiancée's house. A party takes place in the courtyard, with the women singing and ululating. The fiancée's family serves drinks, boiled fava beans, and hard-boiled eggs. There is not a man in sight.

Already we may observe the similarity between this sequence and the ritual of the *'utriya*. But several significant differences must also be noted. Thus, for example, the women of the groom's household have also brought the bride an omelet made from four eggs, which she is the first to taste, together with some homemade bread and a bottle of wine. The feast continues with hard-boiled eggs and fava beans. These foods—and the innumerable plates of couscous that circulate between the spouses' households and among surrounding households—symbolize fecundity and abundance. They are present throughout the cycle. Even if they were not as persistent a feature in the ritual of Nefta, they appear frequently nonetheless in the practices of southern Tunisia and more generally throughout the Maghreb. The Jews of Jerba do not claim to give a religious explanation for these practices. The explanation regularly given is that these are prophylactic measures—"they bring good luck"—and that they have always been followed.

The first evening is called *lailat at-tshamna* (night of fattening), marking the end of a period of several weeks during which the bride was force-fed in order for her to reach a desirable buxom state by the time of the marriage. The theme of fertility remains central on the second evening, called *'ajīn* (night of the raised dough, or of kneading). Previously, the fiancée's family has sent the first counter-gifts to the fiancé's family: an omelet for him and a plate of couscous for the family. In the evening, the gathering takes place at the girl's house; once again, only women and girls participate. The bride sits and holds court, attired in a long-sleeved robe and completely covered by a piece of silk. Only one eye and her arms remain visible. The groom's mother tears off a sleeve of the robe and raised dough is applied to the fiancée's arms and legs.

How do the participants themselves explain their gestures? First on aesthetic grounds: the dough is intended to make the girl's skin white and smooth. But it may be noted that this second stage of preparing the body of the bride remains the responsibility of the groom's mother. She is the one who kneads and molds the fiancée, just like the bread that she makes in her home every day. Similarly, it is the groom's sisters who stay closest to their future sister-in-law: this remains the case most often throughout the entire wedding cycle, as they press their care upon her with jealous attention. There is therefore an appropriation of the girl by the female members of the fiancé's household. They fatten her and give her appropriate shape before allowing him possession.

While this night of the raised dough has no exact equivalent in Nefta, one should point to the similarity between this ritual and that of the depilation for which until recently clay was used for the body and a mixture of fava beans and eggs for the face. In Nefta also, this treatment is considered to give the girl a radiant complexion and smooth skin. But one could hardly imagine a more explicit metaphor than that of the modeling of clay. And the association of fava beans and egg reiterates the theme of fertility, which is ever present in the Jewish wedding celebration.

The women do find—at last—a reference to religion in the fact that the fiancé's mother tears away a sleeve of the fiancée's robe during this night of the raised dough. At issue is the remembrance that even in the midst of rejoicing the Jews must mourn the destruction of the Temple and the loss of their land. Orthodoxy does not require this motif, but it is known to be widespread in the ceremonial of Jewish weddings. We shall return to this later.[10] In the case of Jerba, one cannot refrain from adding another interpretation: the tearing refers to the piercing of the hymen, and it is significant that the fiancé's mother should still be in charge of this operation.

We will not linger over the third sequence of the nuptial cycle. Once the fiancée's family has sent a ring-shaped pastry and a sorghum bread, a feast takes place in the fiancé's house. All the men are absent. Only the women and girls participate in the feast, which is accompanied by singing and the consumption of hard-boiled eggs. As for the fiancée, she has not left her room and thus does not take part in this episode.

The fourth sequence constitutes the "little henna," and takes place on Thursday evening. Essentially it corresponds to the *kiswa* ceremony observed in Nefta. A procession, consisting of the groom's father, some professional musicians, and the girls and women of the household, sets out from the groom's house. They move toward the bride's house, carrying baskets of sweets and henna that will be used during the coming days, and the dress and slippers that the bride will wear for her ritual bath. The procession comes to a halt in front of the bride's home. The groom's mother takes the baskets from her husband and brings them to the room where the girl is seated. The girl then jumps over the baskets seven times.

The feast that follows is double, with men and women of both families participating. However, it takes place at the bride's house. Only the groom is kept away. As for the rest of the men, they are gathered in the courtyard around tables. A meal is served to them while the musicians play Arab music. In the women's quarters, the bride has been dressed and adorned by her future sisters-in-law and the other women. A couscous is served. Then, toward midnight the music grows quicker, and tension mounts in the courtyard. The women lead the veiled bride there, and her father lifts her onto a table. Standing or lifting themselves up on chairs, the girls surround her, carrying lighted candles. Men and women then pass by one by one in line, leaving a gold coin on the tips of her outstretched fingers. Energetic music accompanies this entire ballet. Finally, to conclude this soirée, the groom's mother ties strings to the tips of the bride's fingers and applies henna to them, thus signifying that henceforth the girl belongs to the family of the husband-to-be.

This exhibition of the bride recalls the corresponding episode of the *dukhla*, which in Nefta preceded the consummation of the marriage. Although the offering of gold coins did not occur in the particular case we described, the practice is attested in numerous other ethnographic descriptions from this region.

In Jerba the denouement of the action does not immediately follow this episode. It is postponed, and the ceremonial is as it were suspended for the following two days. Because of the Sabbath, no marriage ritual can take place on Friday and Saturday evenings, except that henna is again applied to the limbs of the bride. On Sunday, the celebrations regain their intensity. In the morning the bride undergoes depilation of the body and the face. Late in the afternoon, her future sisters-in-law come to dress her and adorn her with jewels. In the evening the ceremony of the "great henna" takes place. This marks the high point of the entire cycle. While a tone of restraint, indeed a real gravity, had characterized the previous gatherings, on this occasion joy is openly expressed. This public ceremony, which takes place in the bride's home, brings together not only the families of neighbors and relatives, but also Muslim friends. The groom's mother plays a central role. She arrives dressed in silk and adorned with jewels. She grinds the henna in public and, while she does this, must swallow a hard-boiled egg and drink some alcohol. She jumps over the henna grindstone seven times. The celebration then proceeds with the same gestures as during the "little henna": the bride bows seven times before the henna; she is exhibited and receives offerings of gold coins. Men and women mingle at this party in the presence of professional musicians, who play Arab music. To conclude the festivities, a bit of henna applied to the bride's fingers is carried in procession to the groom's house and applied to his fingers.

The following day, Monday, the bride is delivered to the care of an experienced woman who applies henna three times over to her hands and feet, until these attain a deep brown color. The groom's family prepares the meal for the bride's family, and during the evening the women come to grind spices at her house. All the women participating in the wedding then stain their fingers with henna. This is all that happens on Monday evening.

Before noon on Tuesday, the girl is led to the ritual bath by the married women of her entourage. The unmarried girls who have kept her such close company up to this point are excluded. After immersing herself in the communal *mikveh,* the bride dons the robe and slippers she had previously received. Next she reenters her house, still covered. Her fiancé's family has sent the meal that she takes with those closest to her. It is on this very day and in her house that the marriage contract is drawn up, in the presence of scribes and witnesses.[11] The evening is marked by a great public celebration in the presence of both men and women, this time in the husband's house. As an overture to this *lailat at-tajmīl,* the girl's family sends a dish of couscous to the groom's family as soon as night has fallen. The dish is taken into the open air and eaten under an olive tree, while musicians play secular music. The groom passes through a ritual separation resembling that which his bride has undergone. During the day he has withdrawn from his normal pursuits into the company of men of his own age group.

The ceremonial that follows on this evening is symmetrical to the ceremonial of the great henna, with the groom now being the object of the greatest care. The feast takes place at his house. Henna is applied to him, and above all, he dons the turban. Next, as he remains seated in the middle of a room, his father and then, in turn, the other men wind a red turban around his head, and then quickly remove it. Women may also enter the room and participate in this game through which, with great merriment, the groom is symbolically invested with the attributes of an adult male and of the head of his own household. As for the rest of the ceremony, everything recalls that which took place earlier in the bride's house during the "great henna," including the mixed presence of men and women, of Muslim friends, the performance of secular music and singing, and the distribution of drinks and food. During this same soirée, the bride's family—the bride herself now being absent—enters the section of the house intended for the spouses and drives in some nails, symbolizing that the bride is now securely fixed in her new quarters.

Finally, on Wednesday we reach the last sequence of the wedding celebration that leads to the high point of the entire cycle—*lailat sab'a brakhūt*, "the night of the seven blessings." This sequence clearly recalls the *dukhla* of the Nefta wedding, since the spouses are, at last, united. At the same time, it brings together the most specifically Jewish motifs.

To begin with, the bride is placed in the care of a *ziyyāna*—the "beautifying" woman, who devotes several hours to arranging her coiffure, applying makeup, and preparing her toilette. On the groom's side, the family has been laboring since the early hours of the morning. The meat of a freshly sacrificed animal is prepared for the evening celebration, as are numbers of other special dishes. The groom and his companions decorate the facade of his house and the doorposts of the nuptial chamber with motifs painted in blue. Some of the images are intended to ward off the evil eye—an open band, rows of fish—while others symbolize the two spouses and evoke the memory of the Holy Temple of Jerusalem. The latter consists of two symmetrical candelabra (menorahs) sketched on each side of the main entrance to the groom's house.

At sunset, a moment of intense collective emotion ensues, accompanied by the noisy movement of the crowd and the musicians. This occurs when the young woman leaves the seclusion she has maintained for the preceding ten days, to be slowly led to the house of her bridegroom. She takes this journey on foot, entirely veiled, with musicians and the menfolk of her family leading the procession. The young woman herself is guided and surrounded by a crowd of women and girls and followed by all those who are in one way or another connected to the celebration. The bride makes several stops on her way, each marked by an explosion of ululations and a shower of candy and sweets, which are immediately pounced upon by the swarms of children.

Once the procession arrives at the groom's house, it comes to a halt. The groom, standing on the roof with his best men, pushes off a large, empty ceramic jar, which is supposed to shatter on impact with the ground (if the first jar does not break, he repeats the action). The bride, her hand guided by a sister-in-law, then breaks a raw egg on the right doorpost and enters the courtyard of the house. The groom throws a second jar, this time filled with water, into the courtyard. The bride breaks yet another egg, on the doorpost of the bridal chamber. Finally she enters that room and remains.

As for the groom, a last series of rituals of separation precedes his encounter with the bride. On Tuesday evening he began a twenty-four-hour fast. He must now have his hair cut in the courtyard of the house. Next his companions take him into his best man's house, where he is dressed. Once he has returned home, he is arrayed in his father's prayer shawl, and the men all go together to the synagogue for the evening prayer. Afterward, they form a circle and dance around the groom and lead him back to his home. After pronouncing a blessing, he enters the room where his fiancée is seated, still veiled and invisible. He places the wedding ring on her finger and immediately returns to the courtyard. There, with his head covered by the prayer shawl, he receives the nuptial blessing. The rabbi, with his hand on the groom's head, reads the seven *berakhot* (prayers). The groom takes a sip of the wine that he holds in his hand, then brings the glass to his bride, who is still kept apart and veiled. The bridegroom's mother then quickly lifts her veil; she also takes a sip of wine in her turn; and the husband leaves once again. The bridegroom's mother unveils the bride. She is at last open to view, but remains in her room, where she will share a meal with other women. Although the group of women overflows into the courtyard, it still keeps its distance from the crowd of men.

Once the husband has returned to the courtyard, he sits down at a table with the other men and breaks the fast that he began the preceding night. An abundant meal is provided for the men. The orchestra plays only *piyyutim*, religious melodies. There are no Muslim guests at this final celebration.

A happily married woman is designated to instruct the bride on what is about to take place. The guests withdraw and the couple are left alone in the marriage chamber where the marriage is consummated. The blood-stained nightgown of the bride will be shown to witnesses the next morning. During the twelve following days, sexual relations are suspended since the rupture of the hymen (defloration) has rendered the wife impure. She will also have to go to the ritual bath before resuming sexual contact with her husband. No similar prohibition is current among Muslims.

We stop here and will forego any description of the ritual of reintegration of the new couple into the community. We will instead highlight the contrasts and the similarities between the two rituals considered here.

Socially, an inviolable boundary separates Jews and Muslims in all matters related to marriage. No women can be exchanged between the two communities. An absolute prerequisite for the two ceremonies we have just described is the Muslim identity of both parties in the first case and the Jewish identity in the second. If this condition is not met, the marriage is quite simply impossible. Thus the ascription to one or another group determines the very possibility of an alliance. In Jerba we did not observe a single case violating this rule of endogamy—neither in current practice nor for the period of approximately one century for which we have archival records. I emphasize this point, because in certain recent studies on ethnicity in the Middle East, some authors have asserted that ethnic and religious identity is but one of many options at the disposal of individuals, to be used in the social transactions in which they are constantly engaged, according to the context in which they find themselves.[12] These authors end by losing sight of the fact that ascription to one or another community excludes a certain number of fundamental practices—most notably marriage—from any negotiation whatsoever.

Once again, almost all the persons participating in the entire celebration belong to the same religious community as the couple. The only exceptions occur on those evenings to which members of the other religious groups are invited.

In the series of events that unfold throughout the cycle, the consistent separation of men from women, the more active role of the latter, and the seclusion of the bride (more emphatic in the case of the Jerban Jewish marriage than in that of Nefta) are elements common to both the Jewish and Muslim weddings.

From the point of view of the organization of the ritual, a number of analogies have emerged in the course of our description. We will summarize them only briefly here. The major sequences of the Muslim and the Jewish wedding cycle correspond to each other; motifs present in the one are present in the other. Such is the case, for example, of the clay and paste in which the brides are covered, or the seven circles walked by the Muslim bride and the seven leaps made by the Jewish bride, as well as the meals and other exchanges between the two parties to the marriage. Similarly, the high points of the cycle are identical: the ritual bath, the henna ceremony, the transfer of the bride to the house of the groom, and, of course, the consummation of the marriage.

The strictly religious motifs are limited to the text of the contract, the prayers and songs, although in the Jewish case even some of these are of a profane character. While the young Muslim girl does make one sortie to visit a marabout before the marriage, her Jewish counterpart does not leave her seclusion even once. Nevertheless, a number of specifically Jewish themes in the Jerban wedding should be noted. In particular, the repeated references to the destruction of the Temple of Jerusalem constitute a sort of script within a script of the marriage. At the very moment when a new family is being formed, it prepares itself to perpetuate Jewish life, to be ready to rebuild the Temple. First, the tragedy of the destruction of the Temple is recalled: the gown of the bride is torn, a candle is lit at her bedside on the nights preceding the marriage, and all dancing is forbidden throughout the celebrations (indeed, in the village of Hara Sghira, even musical instruments are forbidden and only singing is permitted). At a later stage, the marriage gives expression to a messianic hope: the two candelabra painted on the doorposts of the marriage house make the young couple into pillars of the Temple to be rebuilt.

Two details of the ritual seem to have as their "historic roots" (to borrow the phrase used by Vladimir Propp in connection with popular tales) in the Jewish condition in Muslim lands.[13] While the Muslim bride was until very recently transported on a litter—and is currently transported by car—the Jerban Jewish bride makes her way to the home of the groom on foot. This is undoubtedly because the Jews, whose *dhimmi* status in Tunisia lasted until the middle of the nineteenth century, could not use any "noble" mounts. Thus, they continued to enshrine as a tradition a practice that had its origins in a prohibition. Similarly, Jews were not permitted to carry arms. And undoubtedly for this reason the Jewish men, unlike their Muslim counterparts, do not fire any salvos at different points in the processions.

In spite of these differences, there is a marked convergence between the practices of the two groups. How is this to be explained?

1. This similarity is not institutional in origin. The law of personal status remains a sphere in which the state does not intervene. It has always been explicitly understood and accepted that these aspects of life were to be governed by the law and by the representatives of the Jewish community.

2. In spite of the spatial segregation between Jews and non-Jews in Jerba, which lasted until the middle of this century, there were always mediators between the self-enclosed community and its Muslim neighbors. Traditionally, the shopkeepers and peddlers who used to sell the henna, spices, notions, and textiles used for the Muslim wedding ceremonies were all Jews. Similarly all the jewelers in southern Tunisia were Jews, and it was often the Jews who furnished the musicians for the various celebrations connected with Muslim weddings. In more recent times, with the expanding local forms of westernization, Jewish seamstresses have been hired to prepare the clothing for the wedding, as well as the curtains and other items for the new household. One can assume that these modest go-betweens played a role in transmitting information about what is done or should be done and about fashions and tastes. A common style thus took shape through these smaller exchanges.
3. More broadly, and again in spite of the spatial segregation and of women's seclusion, both communities lived in contiguity for centuries, with a shared history and equivalent access to the local resources—material as well as symbolic—that resulted in common cultural patterns and practices.

This is a case of cultural symbiosis between two populations, such that it is impossible to trace when local customs were invented and by whom. Instead, we are dealing with a collective anonymous construct, a tradition that everybody accepts, enacts, and transmits. What is considered as authentically Jewish or Muslim is not orthodoxy in the religious sense, but orthodoxy vis-à-vis local norms. In this respect, while it is true that Muslims and Jews did not exchange women, their marriage patterns illustrate the continual mingling of their cultural practices.

NOTES

1. Abraham L. Udovitch and Lucette Valensi, *The Last Arab Jews: the Communities of Jerba, Tunisia* (New York, 1984); Lucette Valensi, "La Tour de Babel: groupes et relations ethniques au Moyen Orient et en Afrique du Nord," *Annales, E.S.C.* 4 (July–Aug. 1986): 817–38.

2. The following observations are based (1) on an on-site inquiry carried out in Jerba, especially in 1978 and 1979 (see Udovitch and Valensi, *Last Arab Jews*); (2) on interviews with Jewish families of Jerba and Muslim families of

the Jerid, now living in Paris; (3) on Keren Friedman, "A 14-day Wedding Celebration: Hara Kebira, The Island of Djerba, Tunisia" (unpublished paper, Department of Anthropology, UCLA, n.d.). Marriage in North Africa, and in particular in southern Tunisia, has given rise to an abundant bibliography. See especially Gilbert Boris, *Documents linguistiques et ethnographiques sur une région du Sud tunisien (Nefzaoua)* (Paris, 1951), chap. 8; Daniel Bruun, *The Cave Dwellers of Southern Tunisia* (London, 1898), chap. 10; Maurice Gaudefroy-Demombynes, "Coutumes de mariage: Algérie," *Revue des traditions populaires* 22 (Feb.–Mar. 1907): 49–60; Harvey Goldberg, "The Jewish Wedding in Tripolitania: A Study in Cultural Sources," *The Maghreb Review* 3:9 (1978): 1–6; André Louis, *Nomades d'hier et d'aujourd'hui dans le Sud tunisien* (Aix, 1979), chap. 9; Edward Westermarck, *Marriage Ceremonies in Morocco* (London, 1914). I especially wish to thank A. and R. Gabbous for sharing their knowledge and pictures with me.

3. Lucette Valensi and Nathan Wachtel, *Mémoires juives* (Paris, 1986).

4. Edward Shils, *Center and Periphery: Essays in Macrosociology* (Chicago, 1975). I retain Shils's definition of tradition, although I do suggest that tradition is constantly being brought up to date. But this is not the place to develop this argument.

5. On matrimonial transactions and the innumerable difficulties that they brought about, see Valensi and Wachtel, *Mémoires juives*, esp. 102–15.

6. For a study that treats the same questions—how to understand Jewish practices within the context of a constant interaction with the Muslim population—but takes a different approach that leads to different conclusions, see Goldberg, "Jewish Wedding in Tripolitania," 1978.

7. See A. J. Greimas, forward to Joseph Courtes, *Introduction à la sémiotique narrative et discursive* (Paris, 1976).

8. Arnold Van Gennep, *The Rites of Passage* (Chicago, 1960).

9. For a brief description of the symbolism of space and time among the Jews of Jerba, see Udovitch and Valensi, *Last Arab Jews*.

10. Here we must remind the reader of the importance of the wedding theme in Jewish mysticism, in which the communities of Jerba are profoundly steeped. For a general interpretation, see Gershom Scholem, *Major Trends in Jewish Mysticism*, 8th ed. (New York, 1974). For an example of the realization of these beliefs during the celebration of Lag ba'omer, see Udovitch and Valensi, *Last Arab Jews*, 121f.

11. The time and place of the signing of the contract are not fixed. The *ketubbah* can, in fact, be signed at the rabbinical school on the Tuesday preceding the night of the seven prayers.

12. See Dale F. Eickelman, *The Middle East: An Anthropological Approach* (Englewood Cliffs, N. J., 1981); Lawrence Rosen, *Bargaining for Reality: The Construction of Social Relations in a Muslim Community* (Chicago, 1984).

13. Vladimir Propp, *Morphology of the Folktale* (Austin, Tex., 1968); idem, *Les racines historiques du conte populaire* (Paris, 1983).

From a Muslim Banquet to a Jewish Seder:

Foodways and Ethnicity Among North African Jews

Joëlle Bahloul

THE ANTHROPOLOGICAL analysis of relationships between Jews and Arabs offers several specific insights for human sciences. First and foremost, these relationships are considered a "whole social fact":[1] they are involved in the total organization of social exchanges and in a wide variety of social processes. In this dyadic interaction, each community displays its own social identity and its perception of its neighbor. Ethnic distinction is analyzed in the cultural sphere, in the political realm, and in economic life. The ethnographic description of daily exchanges in neighborhood relationships should encompass the complex unfolding of an apparently systematic opposition.

Second, considering the Judeo-Arabic relationships as a whole social process, the ethnographic approach strives to capture the particular and private practices and exchanges in which it is involved. For example, ethnography suggests that this dyadic interaction might be found in the material and concrete acts of home life. Thus, even domestic privacy is delineated by ethnic boundaries; as such it is a significant setting for the "politics" of ethnic and religious distinction and contributes to the social definition of the ethnic group.[2]

Within this private domain, social anthropologists have analyzed and explored their social function in particular cultural systems. The major contributions have been provided by the structuralist school, following in the footsteps of Claude Lévi-Strauss. The theoretical model has been found in his famous book *The Origins of Table Manners*,[3] in which cooking practices are deciphered to reveal particular structures that relate to the entire social and cultural order. According to Lévi-Strauss, the wide variety of cooking techniques is actually composed of three major categories: the raw, the cooked, and the rotten, which basically signify the binary opposition between "nature" and "culture." The raw is placed in the category of nature; the cooked is the *cultural* transformation of the raw; and the rotten, its *natural* transformation.

In a certain sense, the cooked symbolizes the culture of the community. The British anthropologist Mary Douglas has analyzed food taboos in the Hebrew tradition from this perspective, employing anthropological interpretation of biblical rules. According to Douglas these taboos constitute an ordering of the material, social, and even cosmic world through the basic opposition between *kasher* and *taref*, clean and unclean. Kosher animals, that is, edible and clean animals, are those whose anatomic and physiological characteristics are in harmony with the Hebrew cosmic order. Nonkosher animals are embodied expressions of disorder: anomalies, monsters in a certain sense. Mary Douglas shows in her analysis to what extent Jewish foodways are affected by the religious, social, and cultural Hebrew system and how they constitute a significant field for social and cultural distinction between Jews and their neighbors. One may find a very similar approach in the work of Louis Dumont and other Indianists who analyze the caste system as a boundary-building system, especially when it deals with rigorous food taboos. In the Indian system, food is clearly a factor in the social and ethnic hierarchy.

Finally, the French, so-called *Annales*, school of social history has striven to show how history is involved in foodways, how food habits offer a source for historical research, and how history is *made* in food practices.

Within this multidisciplinary perspective, I have attempted to analyze the social history of contemporary Algerian Jewish ethnicity through an ethnological survey of food habits.[4] The complexity of this social history lies in what could be considered its double ascription. The contemporary experience of Algerian Jews is characterized by a deep entrenchment both in the Maghrebian history and culture dominated by Islam and in the Hebrew tradition. This characteristic might certainly be extended to include other North African Jewish communities. But the Algerian community was demarcated at the end of the nineteenth century, when it was given French citizenship. As a result it became irreversibly committed to the republican and emancipationist French society. The colonial system at work in Algeria until its independence nurtured this commitment to such a degree that even the abrogation of the Crémieux Decree during the Vichy regime did not weaken it.[5]

In this particular historical context, the study of domestic practices, and of food habits in particular, is relevant because it explains the cultural stakes involved in the semantics of daily and material acts. From this point of view, Judeo-Arabic relationships constitute a process of communication that is neither absolute hostility nor harmonious symbiosis, but an everyday exchange in which each community molds its status vis-à-vis its neighbors. It is a double process that involves (1) the integration of elements of the other culture in its own cultural code and (2) the preservation of specific cultural traits performed as distinctive items. Speech of ethnicity, as expressed in material acts, is altogether a speech of identity and distinction; it requires a shared mode of communication (the same language or the same cultural code) and results in the presence of the Other in the core of the Self culture. My purpose in this article is to analyze Judeo-Arabic relationships as they are *perceived* and culturally articulated in food practices of Algerian Jews. I am suggesting an *inside* approach to the issue, one that focuses on intercommunity relationships as perceived by the Jewish culture.[6]

Before entering the core of the ethnographic articulation of the process, two remarks need to be made about the practical "policy" of Algerian Judeo-Arabic relationships. The first concerns the symbolic articulation of this dyadic interaction in Jewish culture. In fact, a binary relationship in colonial Algerian society was transformed into a triangular one: any interaction between Arabs and Jews was inscribed in a triad of Jews, Christians, and Muslims. In other words, to become a French citizen during the emancipation process, the Algerian Jew had to distinguish himself from the Arab population, culture, and language—the indigenous element par excellence to which the Jew did not want to belong. As in other colonial societies, the adoption of the native community by the dominant culture perforce provoked the divorce of the community from the rest of the indigenous population(s). To this end, French colonial administration had no trouble exploiting a strategy of division.

The second remark deals with the material distinction between

Arabs and Jews in colonial Algeria. Religious and ritual life has been the most significant field for the marking of ethnic differentiation. This mechanism—older than colonialism itself in North African society—survived into the contemporary period. The logic of "otherness" was best communicated in the domain of sacred practices. This is particularly true when one deals with food habits that are, for both communities, governed by a religious and legal code. Moreover, these rules mainly affect edible *meats*: they transform meat consumption into a celebration of ritual sacrifices. The ethnic dimension of meat consumption peaked during Muslim or Jewish festivals, which were, until recent times, practically the only opportunities for meat to appear on the menu. Because vegetables are not affected by religious taboos for either Jews or Muslims,[7] they usually constituted a practical field for cultural encounter, through common terminologies, common cooking techniques, and sometimes common ritual usage of herbs, cereals, and legumes.

Thus, the first part of this paper will analyze the ethnic distinction inscribed in Arab and Jewish meat consumption, while the second part will use the ethnographic description of Algerian Jewish foods to show how edible plants straddle boundaries.

Animals as Boundary Keepers

According to Mary Douglas's structural analysis of Hebrew food taboos, nonkosher and nonedible animals are those that constitute anomalies in the Hebrew cosmological order: imperfection, in other words, is not supposed to be Hebrew. The order that excludes animal anomalies confers a prestigious status on certain species, among which one finds quadruped mammals. These need to be cloven-hoofed ruminants. Bovines and ovines are thus viewed as exemplary animals because they are endowed with anatomic and physiological characteristics of non-flesh-eating animals. The omnivorous pig is anomalous and thus unclean; he has a cloven hoof but is not a ruminant.

The foodways of Algerian Jews offer a subtle illustration of these basic biblical principles. If one questions these Jews about what they consider to be *meat*, they will inevitably concur that it is beef flesh: *beef* is intended when one speaks about meat; beef is meat par excellence. In a certain sense, it constitutes the perfect example of the kosher quadruped mammal. From a quantitative point of view, it is certainly the most frequently consumed meat in Algerian Jewish households. From a qualitative point of view, the way it is cooked and eaten also indicates that it is endowed with a prestigious status within the wide range of kosher meats.

First and foremost, beef is a component of almost all meals of religious holidays. In some cases, it is mandatory, for the Sabbath meal in particular, and might be exclusive in other cases. No other meat can be displayed in certain Sabbath dishes. One should not cook the *tfina*, the traditional Sabbath rich stew, with a cut of mutton or even with lamb. The usual meat for this dish is beef: one may therefore use a cut of veal, since as a bovine flesh, it preserves the exemplary meat category in the semantics of Sabbath cooking. The couscous eaten at Friday dinners is rarely cooked with lamb or with any mammal flesh other than beef. It could be cooked with chicken but culinary semantics would then shift to a different animal category and thus to different conditions of edibility. In sum, among quadruped animals, beef is the perfect animal for ritual and for sacrifice as well. It is the sacred meat, designed for religious meetings.

As a result of this sacrificial function of beef flesh, this "prestigious" meat is endowed with a highly convivial function. It is the meat most frequently consumed at family gatherings and *inside the home*. It is as if the association between beef and holiness aimed to sanctify the closest kinship relations, which are mandatory for ritual celebrations. The symbolic result of this association is the assignment of beef to home gatherings. By eating beef, the family signifies its willingness to withdraw into the universe of its traditional culture. Even families that are not ritual observers would not consider eating a cut of pork or rabbit for the Sabbath dinner. Pork and rabbit are classified in a symbolic category that is radically opposed to that of beef.

Finally, the very distinction of beef consumption is emphasized by the cooking mode assigned to this prestigious flesh. Beef is frequently cooked in rich stews that require slow and long cooking; it is rarely broiled for ritual meals. The holiness of ritual cooking seems to be loosely associated with well-cooked food, and mainly with beef. Accordingly, the exemplary meat is opposed to lamb and mutton, which are ritually broiled for Passover meals, for example (these meals are usually located on the periphery of the celebration: they are scheduled for the lunch preceding the *seder*[8] or following the end of the week of dietary restrictions).

The opposite number of the beef pattern is pork—rarely cooked *inside* the home and eaten raw most of the time, that is, in a ham form or in any other form that does not require home cooking. Through this symbolic procedure, nonobservant families would express their wish to keep their home *closed* to the unclean animal, the pot here symbolizing the home. If we return to the Lévi-Strauss culinary triad, we would then classify beef in the category of the cooked, thus in the realm of culture, the culture of the origins. Mutton, pork, and rabbit would be ranged in the category of the symbolic raw, thus *outside* the culture and tradition of the origins that are celebrated by well-cooked foods.[9] What is significant then in the symbolic procedure that imbues beef with the prestigious status and relegates mutton to the periphery of Algerian Jewish foodways? (1) When speaking of mutton, one would certainly disdain both its "strong" taste and its smell. Moreover, mutton is given a marginal position because it is supposed not to be easily digested. In a certain sense, mutton is placed among "unclean" animals, although it is considered kosher by biblical rules. (2) As opposed to the beef pattern, mutton is almost always excluded from ritual meals, such as the Sabbath meal. And (3) mutton is opposed to beef by the way it is cooked: it rarely appears in stews and is not a well-cooked meat. Symbolically, it is the neighbor of pork, especially when one says of mutton that it is an "Arabic" meat, or, rather, the meat designed for Muslim sacrifices, mainly the *'Id-El-Kbir*. Therefore, because mutton is endowed with this ritual function in the Muslim calendar, it was—and still is—excluded from the Algerian Jewish food calendar. The ritual of the Other places mutton on the margins of the ritual of the Self. Moreover, it symbolizes the indigenous food par excellence, food consumed by indigenous populations from which the Jews in Algeria wished to distinguish themselves as they became progressively more westernized.

In Algerian Jewish cuisine, the symbolic articulation of the three meats—beef, mutton, and pork—encompasses the triangular relationship between Jews, Muslims, and Christians in colonial society. Food habits tend to demonstrate here how material acts trace ethnic boundaries. In the Algerian Jewish code, beef is the keeper of the internal, a boundary never straddled. Pork and mutton, located outside this boundary, manage intercommunity communication. Finally, meats of different animals appear as boundary keepers (see figure 1).

This symbolic system should be analyzed within the historical context of contemporary colonial Algeria: emancipated Jews improved their way of life and, as a result, increased their consumption of expensive food products, like meat. In the process they were likely to

Figure 1. Food as Symbolic Articulation of Boundaries

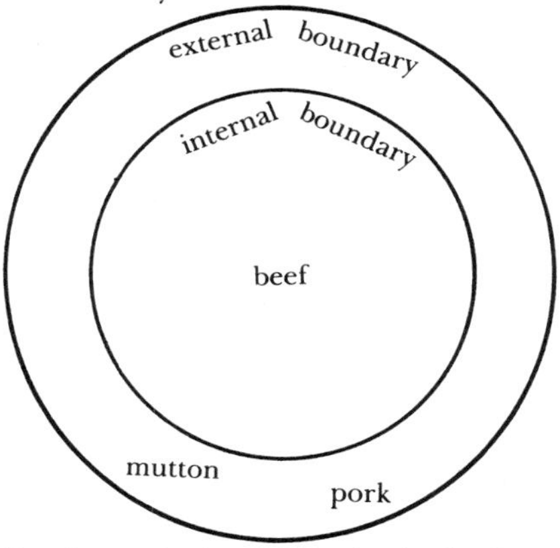

abandon Hebrew food restrictions, particularly those related to meat selection. This erosion of traditional customs was most striking among the Jewish upper classes. The higher the social status, the weaker the food restrictions. As Jews moved up the social ladder, they became assimilated, at least ideologically, to French social values, and they progressively withdrew from the indigenous society. The indigenous, and thus "traditional" element par excellence, was Muslim. Therefore, what appeared as an ethnic differentiation in meat consumption was actually performed as a form of social emancipation. In this complex articulation, Algerian Jewish foodways display the triangular structure of the dyadic relationship between Arabs and Jews in colonial North Africa.

The Vegetable Grammar

Hebrew dietary laws deal in part with vegetables, which are not subject to the systematic type of biological conditions that are imposed on edible meats. The Mediterranean background is probably more significant than are religious rules for understanding Algerian Jewish foodways regarding edible plants. In their consumption of vegetables, Algerian Jews testify to their deep participation in North African popular culture. One might find an illustration of this process in the symbolic use of couscous and of all foods having a seedlike texture—those foods that usually symbolize fertility, fecundity, and wealth in popular beliefs. This material semiology encompasses two other semantic terms: color and flavor. Sweet foods and green foods are considered beneficent and are eaten in major rituals generally located at the transition between two cycles: the Sabbath, the eve of the New Year, and the Passover seder. Couscous, sweet pastries, or spinach stews are the appropriate beneficent foods for a wedding or a bar mitzvah,[10] that is, for the major life-cycle "rites of passage," which are rich in community and family blessings. This popular semiology does not constitute a particularly Jewish characteristic in North African society; it is found as well in other Mediterranean cultures and popular rites. What is more significant of the cultural relationship between local Arabs and Jews is the mutual acculturation of popular ritual semantics in each culture. The ritual for the eve of the New Year, the Rosh Hashanah meal, offers a relevant illustration of this process.

According to the *Shulḥan 'Arukh*,[11] that ritual must be governed by two basic principles. First, it has to be convivial, celebrated by a gathering of the extended family. It must be joyous and present aesthetic foods. In sum, it should perform on the table a dramatization of wealth and blessing for the coming year. The second principle deals with linguistic and taxonomic semantics: Jews should serve for this meal specific foods that are symbolically beneficent in the local language of everyday life; these in turn should suggest relevant Hebrew blessings. Ethnographic examples will clarify this semantic procedure, the aim of which is to build a bridge between food terminology and linguistic terminology.

The Rosh Hashanah meal is opened by a complex succession of benedictions in which the family and its guests taste pieces of seasonal fruits, seeds, or vegetables of the local market while Hebrew blessings are pronounced. Most Jewish families from other parts of the world reduce this tasting ritual to the blessing of apples and honey, bread and wine. North African Jewish families perform a complex ritual composed of the following tastings and blessings: apple, honey, date, fig, pomegranate, sesame, leek, Swiss chard or spinach, squash, green beans, the head of a lamb or a piece of beef cheek. In addition to these blessings, the table scenography should substitute sugar for salt for the blessing of bread. This substitution is supposed to communicate the communal wish for beneficent sweetness, and one says: "Be next year as sweet as the sugar and honey that we eat tonight!" In this vegetable and fruit grammar presented on the table for the blessings, one notices the combination of the three major beneficent symbols in popular North Africa culture: seedlike texture, green color, and sweet flavor.

The *seedlike texture* is represented by pomegranates, sesame seeds, and green beans. They are tasted while pronouncing the Hebrew blessing that displays the word *yarbu*, "proliferate." The seedlike texture is associated with the idea of proliferation that is signified in the Hebrew word. The principle of analogy between food terminology and the blessing terminology should help the taster *eat the word* "proliferation." The taster should literally *incorporate* the idea the blessing word supports.

The *green color* is represented by green beans and by spinach. Green is usually a beneficent color in Muslim popular belief. Fellahs of the eastern Maghreb eat a very green dish of vegetables and spinach for the Muslim new year meal. Similarly Jewish cuisine of these regions includes a green dish of spinach for the Rosh Hashanah meal. Popular beliefs in the eastern Maghreb have been "muslimized" in the new year ritual exactly as they have been "hebraized" in the same ritual of the Jewish calendar.

Finally, the third beneficent element of this food scenography is represented by the *sweet flavor* that dominates the meal, as previously discusssed.

The fruit and vegetable setting offers specific Hebrew symbols as well as popular North African and Muslim symbols that have been hebraized. This is the concrete application of the commandment in the *Shulḥan 'Arukh*, according to which each family should eat at this meal foods considered beneficent in the local language. Moreover, Judeo-Arabic cultural integration might be observed in the semantic exchange, within the ritual, between the linguistic code and its iconographic and taste support. Some examples will clarify this semantic procedure.

Date is called in Arabic *t'mar*. When the eater tastes a date, he/she should pronounce a blessing that includes the Hebrew word *yitamu*, "eradicate our enemies." In fact, while eating the date *(t'mar)*, the eater tastes the word *yitamu* too; he/she eats the "eradication of our enemies." The overlapping of taste and language semantics ends in eating sacred words, in eating text, finally.

Another example illustrating this semantic procedure can be found in the blessing of the spinach, which is called in Arabic *selq*, and blessed by the Hebrew word *yistalqu*, "disappear enemies!" Therefore, while tasting the spinach, the eater actually tastes the blessing word *yistalqu*. The same procedure is repeated for squash and green

Figure 2. Semantic Correspondence Between Food and Words

Vegetable	**Arabic word**	**Hebrew blessing**
date	*t'm*ar	yi*tam*u (eradicate our enemies)
green beans	*rub*iya	yi*rb*u (multiply our good deeds)
spinach	*selq*	yi*sta*l*q*u (disappear our enemies)
squash	*q'ra*	ti*qrā* (God gives his judgment)

beans according to figure 2. One sees that the phonetic analogy between Hebrew and Arabic words lies in the similarity of triliteral roots in both languages.

These fruits and vegetables are familiar products of the North African market, at least in the eastern Maghreb. This subtle ritual procedure incorporates therefore not only the overlapping of taste terminology and language terminology, but the additional overlapping of Arabic and Hebrew words, to such an extent that the eater is helped to the Hebrew word through the Arabic name of the vegetable. The Arabic *lexicon* is here used for the purpose of the Hebrew *syntax*, as recommended in the *Shulḥan 'Arukh*. The integration of Arabic and Jewish cultures is articulated in the unfolding of daily exchanges. The local language—Arabic—allows the social reproduction of the Hebrew ritual code. In daily culture, relationships between Arabs and Jews are communicated in terms of both exchange and ethnic identity: both communities speak the same "language" (in the general cultural meaning of the term), but each speaks it within its particular syntax, which is used to distinguish itself vis-à-vis its neighbor.

NOTES

1. M. Mauss, *The Gift* (Glencoe, Ill., 1954), p. 76.
2. F. Barth, *Ethnic Groups and Boundaries* (Boston, 1969).
3. Cl. Lévi-Strauss, "Short Treatise on Culinary Anthropology," in *The Origin of Table Manners* (London, 1978), pp. 471–95.
4. J. Bahloul, *Le culte de la Table Dressée: Rites et Traditions de la table juive algérienne* (Paris, 1983); for a detailed overview of the current research on Jewish foodways, see idem, "Foodways in Contemporary Jewish Communities: Research Directions," in *Jewish Folklore and Ethnology Review* 9:1 (1987): 1–5.
5. This decree conferred French citizenship on Algerian Jews in 1870.
6. This paper is based on data collected in the late 1970s among Algerian Jewish families established in France. Although the community was no longer

living in an Arab environment, the observed practices *did* perform, in complex arrangements, past relationships with the Arab community in Algeria. In fact, today's practices indicate that forms of social identification in European society have broadcast the terminology of ethnic distinction vis-à-vis the former Arab neighbor.

7. The exception is the prohibition against eating leavened cereals during the week of Passover.

8. The Passover meal, which requires the narration of the flight of the Hebrews from Egypt.

9. Pork and rabbit have been introduced in Algerian Jewish foodways along with some other aspects of French cuisine.

10. Ritual that celebrates male puberty.

11. Code of Jewish law written in the sixteenth century by the famous Sephardic Palestinian rabbi Joseph Caro. This code, amplified by the glosses of his contemporary, the Polish rabbi Moses Isserles, still governs religious practices of traditional Jews.

Contacts and Boundaries in the Domain of Language:

The Case of Sefriwi Judeo-Arabic

Norman A. Stillman

UNTIL THE dissolution of most of the Jewish communities of the Arab world in recent years, perhaps no area of contact and boundary was more indicative of the cultural relation between Jews and Arabs than the domain of language. It was the shared linguistic element that the late S. D. Goitein dubbed "the first and most basic aspect of Jewish-Arab symbiosis."[1] Still, one might be tempted to observe, paraphrasing the well-known witticism vis-à-vis Americans and British, that Jews and Arabs were in a very real sense "divided by a common language."

What I should like to do in this paper* is to take the case of a modern Jewish variety of Arabic as an example of the complexity of cultural conjunction and disjunction. The example is the Judeo-Arabic of Sefrou, Morocco. In order to place Sefriwi Judeo-Arabic within its proper historical and cultural context, it will be necessary to: (1) discuss the notion of Jewish languages in general, (2) briefly survey the development of the Judeo-Arabic phenomenon, (3) fit Sefriwi Judeo-Arabic into the scheme, and (4) describe some of the features of this particular language.

Jewish Languages

The concept of Jewish languages as a classification of a broad group of languages was pioneered by Max Weinreich and Solomon Birnbaum

* Parts of this paper are incorporated into my monograph, *The Language and Culture of the Jews of Sefrou: An Ethno-Linguistic Study*. The Journal of Semitic Studies Monograph Series, no. 11 (Manchester, 1988).

and has been developed in recent years by Herbert Paper, Paul Wexler, and Joshua Fishman.[2] The notion of Jewish languages has been gaining acceptance among students of both linguistics and cultural history as a valuable theoretical and methodological device.

The very existence of numerous Jewish languages has been a function of more than two millennia of Diaspora life, as mitigated or tempered by Jewish group cohesion within the far-flung lands of their dispersion. These languages are a reflection of that dynamic tension in Jewish cultural history between the conflicting urges of assimilation and individuality. As the late Haim Hillel Ben-Sasson has noted, once an initially "alien language gained acceptance, it became not only a vehicle of Jewish cultural and religious creativity, but also gradually became converted into a specifically Jewish idiom and mark of Jewish identity that even formed barriers to later assimilation."[3] I should hasten to add here that the last part of Ben-Sasson's observation regarding these languages as "barriers to later assimilation" has its greatest validity in the case of Germanic Yiddish in its Slavic environment and Romance Ladino in its Turkish, Greek, Slavic, and Arabic milieus, although it does have some validity, too, in the case of Judeo-Arabic in its Muslim Arabic setting.

A common bond links the various Jewish languages belonging to very different linguistic families and also distinguishes them from their non-Jewish cognates. This is the ubiquitous use of Hebrew script for writing them and the inclusion, and indeed ready assimilation, of an element of Hebrew and Aramaic vocabulary (or rather, Hebrew/Aramaic vocabulary, since the tradition makes little distinction between the two and draws upon them as a single source). The element of Hebrew script cannot be dismissed as merely a mechanical difference. In Arabic and Jewish culture, as in many other cultures, script is strongly linked to communal identity, all the more so when the script has a religious sanctity. The parallel cases of Serbian and Croatian and of Hindu and Urdu are cogent examples. The element of Hebrew/Aramaic vocabulary in Jewish language cannot be lightly dismissed either since it points to a very different source for the cultural models than that of non-Jewish cognates.

The Historical Development of Judeo-Arabic

Among the three major Jewish languages of the post-talmudic period (that is, Judeo-Arabic, Yiddish, and Ladino), Judeo-Arabic holds a place of special significance. It has had the longest recorded history—from the ninth century to the present.[4] It has had the widest geographical diffusion—extending across three continents during the Middle Ages. And finally, it was the medium of expression during one of the foremost periods of Jewish cultural and intellectual creativity.

In the wake of the Islamic conquests of the seventh and eighth centuries, Jews from Spain to the border of Iran adopted, along with other peoples, the Arabic language. They did so because Arabic was becoming, as Greek and Aramaic had been before, the international language of the new ecumene, only now over an even larger area.

Prior to the rise of Islam, the only Jews speaking Arabic were the Jewish tribes of the Arabian Peninsula. Their daily language was similar to that of their Arab neighbors save for the admixture of Aramaic and Hebrew words expressing specifically Jewish religious and ethnocultural ideas. The Arabs referred to this early Judeo-Arabic dialect as *al-Yahūdiyya*. Some of the Hebrew and Aramaic terminology of this earliest Judeo-Arabic, as well as a number of religious concepts, passed into the speech of the Arabs at large.[5]

The art of writing was extremely limited in sixth- and seventh-century Arabia. Jews certainly wrote occasional documents in Arabic using Hebrew characters, but they produced no Judeo-Arabic literature. The only Arabic literary form at the time was poetry composed orally according to strict conventions in the supratribal idiom of Classical Arabic. The poems of the Jew al-Samaw'al b. 'Ādiyā', for example, cannot be considered Judeo-Arabic, as they are entirely devoid of Jewish linguistic or conceptual content (criteria that I shall expand upon presently).[6]

With the exception of Yemen and the southernmost part of the Peninsula, which constitute a separate cultural zone, Arabian Jewry disappeared early in the Islamic era. There does not seem to be any organic link between what I would designate Proto-Judeo-Arabic and the Classical Judeo-Arabic of the Middle Ages.[7]

What I have dubbed Classical Judeo-Arabic came into being under the cultural stimulus of the Dār al-Islām, which encompassed the majority of world Jewry at that time, and it developed and flowered with the concomitant rise of medieval Islamic civilization.

By the tenth century Jews from Spain and Morocco in the West to the borders of Iran in the East had begun to use Arabic not only as their daily spoken language, but for nearly all forms of written expression, including religious queries and responsa *(she'ēlōt ū-*

teshūvōt), documents, textual commentaries, philosophical and scientific literature, and day-to-day correspondence. Only poetry was written exclusively in Hebrew during the medieval period. The reason for this last exception was nationalistic: in Islamic civilization poetry was the ultimate national art, a belief that the Jews in the medieval Muslim world thoroughly assimilated. The remark made by Moses b. Ezra in his *Kitāb al-Muḥāḍara wa 'l-Mudhākara* addresses precisely that point:

> Because the Arab tribes excelled in their eloquence and rhetoric, they were able to extend their dominion over many languages and to overcome many nations, forcing them to accept their suzerainty.[8]

Hebrew poetry was cultivated as a national response, an emphatic assertion of the equality of Jewish secular, or national, culture with Arab and Arabic culture. The poet and translator Judah al-Ḥarīzī (d. ca. 1235) states quite candidly that he composed his *Taḥkemōnī* in obvious imitation of the Arabic tour de force, the *Maqāmāt* of al-Ḥarīrī, in order to "show the power of the Holy Language to the Holy People."[9] This was especially important in Islamic Spain, where great emphasis was placed upon religious, linguistic, and racial purity."[10]

But with the exception of poetry for the reasons I have just outlined, Arabic was the primary medium of expression. It was into Arabic that Sa'adya Gaon translated the Hebrew Bible, and it was in that language that he composed his commentary, the *Sharḥ*. It was in Arabic that he wrote the first systematic work on Jewish theology, the *Kitāb al-Amānāt wa 'l-I'tiqādāt* (Book of Doctrines and Beliefs), that Judah Halevi wrote his philosophical dialogue, *The Kuzari*, and that Maimonides wrote his masterful synthesis of Judaism and Aristotelianism, the *Dalālat al-Ḥā'irīn (The Guide of the Perplexed)*.[11]

The Jews in the medieval Muslim world did not write in the spoken dialects of the period, but in Middle Arabic, a form of the language between the Classical Arabic (the only acceptable medium of written expression in Islamic culture) and the local vernaculars. Medieval Judeo-Arabic was essentially a written language that ranged in style from what may be considered Classical Arabic with some Middle Arabic elements to a slightly classicized Middle Arabic bristling with colloquialisms, depending upon the education of the writer and the formal or informal nature of the written material.

Over the past century, a considerable amount of scholarly effort has been devoted to editing, translating, and interpreting medieval Judeo-Arabic literary and documentary texts, especially those from the Cairo Geniza. The language itself has been amply described and its historical development traced, most notably by Joshua Blau.[12]

Medieval Judeo-Arabic began to give way to Modern Judeo-Arabic forms throughout much of the Middle East and North Africa in the late fifteenth century. The main characteristic of the many heterogeneous forms of Modern Judeo-Arabic is its colloquial nature. Jews now wrote, more of less, the same language they spoke (or at least one much closer to the spoken language). The shift from Middle Arabic (the Classical Judeo-Arabic) to modern, communal vernaculars resulted mainly from the increased social isolation of the Jews of the Arab world at the end of the Middle Ages—in many instances within restrictive quarters, such as the mellah and the *ḥārat al-Yahūd*.[13] This physical isolation was never total, even in Morocco and Yemen, where it was most strictly enforced. Socially and psychologically, however, it was almost complete.

The shift from the medieval written language to the modern communal vernaculars also represented in part a decline in the general level of education throughout the Islamic world. The ability to write in Classical Arabic, for example, had seriously deteriorated among Muslims during this period and was only revived with the *Naḥda* (the Arab cultural awakening) movement led by Syrian and Lebanese Christians in the second half of the nineteenth century. This movement, however, held little appeal for the vast majority of the Jews in the Arab world, who did not identify with Arab culture, much less Arab nationalism. (Iraqi Jewry, I should note, was an important exception to this indifference, at least as far as Arabic culture was concerned.)[14]

Dialect forms had already begun to make their appearance in medieval Judeo-Arabic. In many of the Geniza letters written by North Africans or people of North African extraction, the *nf'l/nf'lū* shibboleth of Maghrebi dialects is prevalent.[15] In one Geniza letter from the eleventh century, a Moroccan merchant continually substitutes /z/ for /j/ *(zā'* for *jīm)*, a hallmark today of most urban Judeo-Arabic dialects of northern and central Morocco.[16] In several instances, eleventh-century writers from North Africa drop the prosthetic *alif* of the *af'al* form, giving the typical Maghrebi *f'el* (thus, *ḥdeb* for *aḥdab* and *'ḍem* for *a'ẓam*).[17] Some typically Maghrebi dialect words such as *āsh* and *fāsh* creep in as well. [18] This dialectal substratum becomes our later Judeo-Arabic.

Modern Judeo-Arabic has not elicited the same amount of scholarly attention as has medieval Judeo-Arabic. This is due in part to the fact that there is no single entity comprehended by the term "Modern Judeo-Arabic." It is, rather, a rich multitude of local communal dialects and a lesser number of regional literary languages. This lack of scholarly interest is also due in no small measure to a classicist bias that viewed the intellectual, spiritual, and artistic work of the late Middle Ages and early modern times as essentially decadent. Not untypical is the judgment expressed in the *Encyclopaedia Judaica* article surveying Judeo-Arabic literature, which dismisses everything written after the fifteenth century with the conclusion that "it must be admitted that there is little value in these works, most of which are liturgical, exegetic, or translations of Hebrew pietistic works."[19]

Times, scholarly interests, and even taste change. Popular literature, for example, is now appreciated for its own sake and judged on its own terms. Of late, Judeo-Arabic poetry from Yemen and Morocco has become the subject of study by scholars in Israel, France, and the United States, not only for its ethnographic or linguistic interest but for its aesthetic merit as well.[20] This poetry represents a significant sociological and cultural shift, namely, that in more recent periods Jews in certain parts of the Arab world composed poetry in Arabic, as well as in Hebrew. Much of the Judeo-Arabic poetry employs the forms and motifs of the popular poetry of surrounding Muslim society, which indicates that the social isolation of the late medieval and early modern periods was anything but a hermetic seal, especially on the level of popular and material culture.

My own particular research interest over the past few years—the domain of language as an area of contact and boundary for the Jews in the matrix of an Arab society—led me to the study of a modern form of Judeo-Arabic: the language of the Jews of Sefrou, Morocco. Unlike Haïm Zafrani's recent work on literary Judeo-Moroccan,[21] my own interest has been concerned with the other half of the linguistic picture: the living daily language, the language of speech and thought. This language and various facets of the specific culture it expresses are the subject of my ethnolinguistic monograph on the Jews of Sefrou.[22]

Sefriwi Judeo-Arabic in the Context of Arabic and Judeo-Arabic

The language of the Jews of Sefrou belongs to the great Maghrebi Arabic dialect family that includes varieties spoken from Libya to Morocco and Mauretania, as well as Maltese, and for the Middle Ages Andalusian Arabic.[23] Sefriwi Judeo-Arabic is of the so-called old urban type *(le vieux parler citadin*, as the French linguists refer to it) spoken prior to to the arrival of the Banū Hilāl and Ma'qīl Bedouin in Morocco during the second half of the twelfth century.[24] Hence, it shows many affinities with the varieties of Arabic spoken in Old Fez (Fās al-Bālī) and the Fez Mellah, Taza, Rabat, Sale, Tetuan, and El-Qsar El-Kebir,[25] although it also exhibits certain features of the Jebli, or old montagnard speech (also considered pre-Hilālī) found to the north and east of it.[26]

The question might be posed with some justice: Is the language of the Jews of Sefrou a Jewish language? The problem is philosophical, and its implications are methodological. The French linguist Louis Brunot, who studied the language spoken by the Jews of Fez, makes the blanket assertion with regard to Moroccan Jewish vernaculars that "ils ne sont pas judéo-arabes, mais arabes."[27] Brunot's argument is strengthened by the fact that the various forms of Judeo-Arabic have no particular name comparable to Yiddish, Judezmo, Haketía, or Shuadit, and in fact are generally referred to by the Jews themselves simply as *al-'arabiyya* (Arabic).

Joseph Chetrit, a Moroccan-born linguist who trained in France and is now in Israel, takes a diametrically opposite position:

> En outre, quelle que soit leur origine arabe, les LJA [langues judéo-arabes] du Maroc comme de toute l'AFN [l'Afrique du Nord] sont bel et bien juives.[28]

Chetrit argues with cogency that despite their Arabic matrix, these languages are specifically Jewish because they refer implicitly or explicitly to a well-delineated Jewish sociocultural and sociopsychological universe.[29] In support of Chetrit's position and in contradistinction to Brunot's, it might also be noted that although the Jews have no special name for their language, they do use such terms—in Morocco at least—as *l-'arabiyya dyalna* (our Arabic) when wishing to differentiate between their speech and that of their Muslim neighbors, which is referred to as *l-'arabiyya d-l-msilmīn*. Furthermore, in Fez and Rabat, the Muslims have a term, *lashuniyya* (from Hebrew *lashōn*, "language"), which they use to designate the cognate Jewish language.[30] Chetrit's stance finds support in the work of students of Jewish interlinguistics, such as Birnbaum, Weinreich, Fishman, and Wexler, who approach the phenomenon of Jewish languages as a whole both historically and typologically.[31]

A middle ground in this debate over classification is that taken by the late Haim Blanc, who as a student of Arabic vernaculars preferred the notion of communal dialects. In surveying the sociolinguistic situation in some North African cities, Blanc came to the conclusion that in places such as Algiers, Fez, and Tlemcen—and to these one might certainly add Sefrou—there is what he considered to be "intermediate differentiation" between Muslim and Jewish dialects, "which present, in addition to differences of the minor variety, a number of more strictly structural differences."[32] Blanc's approach to the speech of ethnoreligious groups within the Arabic-speaking world in terms of communal dialects of minor, intermediate, or major differentiation is highly appropriate and far more fruitful from the sociolinguistic standpoint than is Brunot's narrow perspective. It might be justly applied in an analysis of Sefriwi Judeo-Arabic in comparing it with Muslim speech as well as other varieties of Moroccan Judeo-Arabic.

Nevertheless, Sefriwi Judeo-Arabic still must be defined, I believe, as a Jewish language. First, it contains the two essential elements mentioned above at the very outset as linking Jewish languages, even those that may, in and of themselves, have no genetic unity. These are the use of Hebrew script in writing them and the inclusion and easy assimilation of a Hebrew/Aramaic component in the vocabulary. Second, and no less importantly, as Chetrit has pointed out with regard to all the varieties of North African Judeo-Arabic, it is set within a specifically Jewish cultural context, which—I would add—places it in turn within the larger framework of other Jewish languages.[33] These points will be highlighted in the following brief survey of some of the distinguishing features of Sefriwi Judeo-Arabic.

Characteristic Features of Sefriwi Judeo-Arabic

Pronunciation is one of the areas of minor differentiation that sets Sefriwi Judeo-Arabic apart from the neighboring Muslim correlate. The differences include consonants, vowels, and intonation. In Sefriwi

Judeo-Arabic /'/ replaces /q/, /z/ replaces /ž/, and /s/ replaces /š/. In certain positions /k/ is also replaced by /'/. Thus, for example:

> *s-'al-le'* (What did he say to you?)[34]
> *a-saxbar'üm* (How are you?)[35]
> *ha huwa zay* (That's him coming.)[36]

Many of these individual features can be found in some other varieties of Moroccan Arabic, but the combination and the consistency in Sefriwi Judeo-Arabic is unique.

Significantly, the verb system in Sefriwi Judeo-Arabic, as in other Jewish forms of Moroccan Arabic, differs from that used in the language of Muslims. There are differences of inflection: Sefriwi Judeo-Arabic, for example, does not differentiate between first person sing. perf. and second person sing. perf.; nor does it distinguish between second person masc. sing. imperf. and second person fem. sing. imperf.[37] There are differences of form, for example, /kel/ versus /kla/ for "to eat," both ultimately derived from Classical Arabic *akala*. And there is the use of completely different basic verbs, for example, /ra/ for "to see" versus Muslim /šaf/, /nifṭār/ "to pass away" versus Muslim /teweffa/.[38]

Just as Sefriwi Judeo-Arabic uses a number of verbs that differ from those in Muslim Moroccan, so too it employs a considerable number of different nouns, for example, /meṣḥaf/ for "book" (versus /kitāb/), /ḥadīṯa/ for "story" (versus /ḥkāya/), /ṭifoṛ/ for "dish" (versus /ṭabsel/), and /batta/ for "dress" (versus /keswa/.)[39] It also uses different forms of some nouns shared with the Muslim language, for example, /bü/ and /xu/ for "father" and "brother" (versus /ḅḅa/ and /xa/)[40] for /üzih/ and /üziha/ for "face" and "surface" (versus /wežh// and /wžeh/). Plural forms of nouns differ at times. In Sefriwi Judeo-Arabic the plural of /mṛa/ (woman) is /mrawāţ, never the heteroclitic form /'ayalāţ/ commonly used by Muslims.

Sefriwi Judeo-Arabic uses some different pronouns than does the Muslim language. For example, it never employs the relative /əlli/ and /li/, but only /di/.

One of the hallmarks of Sefriwi Judeo-Arabic is its considerable Hebrew vocabulary, although there is nothing near the approximately 4,000 Hebrew lexical items that some have listed for Yiddish.[41] It is difficult to say whether this is indeed because, as my late mentor Professor Goitein has hypothesized, Arabic-speaking Jewry's "knowledge of living Hebrew was far more developed than was the case in eastern Europe" and so "they refrained from mixing up the languages."[42] (But I am not convinced by Goitein's argument.) Moshe Bar-Asher using both contemporary and historical written sources as well as informants from five different regions of Morocco was able to build up a glossary of nearly 2,000 Hebrew words. However, for the Judeo-Arabic of a single region of concentration (the Tafilalt), the maximum number of Hebrew lexical items in the speech of rabbis and scholars was approximately 500, in the speech of literate men 330, and in the speech of illiterate men and women 285 and 260 respectively.[43]

In accordance with what seems to be a general rule in Jewish languages, in Sefriwi Judeo-Arabic Hebrew words take Hebrew plural endings. Thus, /ḥalöm/, /ḥalömöţ/ (dream, dreams); /sim/, simöţ/ (sacred names); /baḥur/, /baḥurim/ (bachelor, bachelors); /ṣeddi'/, /ṣeddi'm/ (saint, saints). Hebrew loan words, however, always take the Arabic definite article /l/ or its appropriate equivalent for words beginning with "sun letters." Thus, we have the forms /l-ereṣ/ (the land of Israel) and /ṣ-ṣeddi'/ (the saint). The sole exception is in compounds or calque phrases in which there is a Hebrew construct or a formula in which the Hebrew definite article occurs, as, for example, /'iddus has-sīm/ (Sanctification of the Divine Name, martyrdom).

Naturally, much of the Hebrew vocabulary is for distinctly Jewish religious or social concepts, as for example, /t-ţōra/ (the Torah), /s-sīfer/ (the Torah scroll), /skka/ (Sukka), /kasīr/ (kosher), /sxüţ/ (blessed merit), /ṭabila/ (ritual immersion), /dine nefasoţ/ (criminal law cases), and /braxa/ (blessing). But Hebrew words are also used for more or less secular concepts (although admittedly the line between religious and secular in Jewish and Islamic North African society is hazy). Examples of this phenomenon are /güf/ (body), /kuwwaḥ/ (strength, force), /gibboṛ/ (a strong person), /ṣara/ (trouble), /gzera/ (calamity), /sa'ar/ (sorrow), /aḥizaţ 'enayim/ (magic illusion), or /ṭiṭos/ (Titus, i.e., something or someone detestable).

Hebrew vocabulary is prominent in Sefriwi Judeo-Arabic blessings and pious expressions such as /sabbaţ salöm/ (Sabbath of Peace), /orex yamim u-snöţ, ḥayim/ (Length of Days and Years of Life, i.e., Mimouna blessing), /sxro l-braxa/ (May his memory be blessed), and /bar minnan/ (God forbid).

Certain Hebrew interjections have become part of the everyday language of men and women, for example, /badday/ (of course!),

/afillu/ (even so), and /barux hab-ba/ (Welcome! and also Suit yourself! or Do as you please).

The Hebrew words that have been incorporated into Sefriwi Judeo-Arabic sometimes take on special meanings that differ from normal Hebrew usage. In Sefrou, as in all of Jewish Morocoo, /me'ara/, which in Hebrew means "cave," signifies "a Jewish cemetery." Other examples of original semantic usages are /l-gifen/ (kiddush wine and the kiddush blessing), /ḥezzān/ (rabbi, scholar), /l-'ölam/ (everything).

A few Hebrew roots have been assimilated into verbs in Sefriwi Judeo-Arabic, for example, /mṣa/, /imṣi/ (to make the blessing over bread, i.e., ha-Mōṣī), /piyyeṭ/ (to sing a religious poem), and /nifṭar/ (to pass away). However, there are religious acts that are also referred to by combining an Arabic verb with a Hebrew noun, for example, /birk l-gifen/ (to recite kiddush), /'era sīma'/ (to recite Shema), /'amal təbiluṭ/ (to immerse oneself in the mikveh), or /ṣeḷḷi 'arabīṭ/ (to perform the evening prayer). This sort of fusion is common in other Jewish languages (cf. Yiddish *maxn kiddəš* and *davenen mayrev*).

One of the hallmarks of male speech is the citation of entire Hebrew phrases in speaking without any translation into Arabic. These quotations are drawn primarily from the Bible, the liturgy, and from rabbinic literature. The following is an excerpt from a story that was told by the shammash, or beadle, of the synagogue in Sefrou to a group of men, women, and children. It illustrates the use of extended Hebrew citations in the speech of educated men:

Hadak Rabbi Smu'el l-Baz - 'alav has-salöm - 'awd l-'ihila d-l-blad. Zaw huma 'alu-lo: Ki birobb halömöt we-habalīm harbē. Had l-ḥaza ma-n'amlü-has.
(That Rabbi Samuel El-Baz—peace be upon him—told [his dream] to the Jewish community of the town. They said to him: "For through the multitude of dreams and vanities are many words."[44] We shall not do this thing.)

No translation of the biblical passage was provided because none was deemed necessary.

The use of Hebrew and, prior to the arrival of the French, of a strong Spanish lexical component indicates the ideal culture models that were considered most important by Moroccan Jews. Jews were very much a part of the Moroccan culture in which they lived, to be sure, but they also differentiated themselves—in a variety of ways, not least among these in the domain of language where the boundaries were continually delineated amidst the contacts.

NOTES

1. S. D. Goitein, *Jews and Arabs: Their Contacts Through the Ages*, 3d rev. ed. (New York, 1974), p. 131.

2. See e.g., S. A. Birnbaum, "Jewish Languages" in *Essays in Honour of the Very Rev. Dr. J. H. Hertz* (London, 1943), pp. 51–67; Max Weinrich, *History of the Yiddish Language* (Chicago, 1980), pp. 45–174; Herbert H. Paper, ed., *Jewish Languages: Theme and Variation* (Cambridge, Mass., 1978); Paul Wexler, "Jewish Interlinguistics: Facts and Conceptual Framework," *Language* 57:1 (1981): 99–149; and Joshua A. Fishman, ed., *Readings in the Sociology of Jewish Languages* (Leiden, 1985).

3. H. H. Ben-Sasson, *Encyclopaedia Judaica* (1972), s.v.. "Assimilation: Antiquity and the Middle Ages."

4. The oldest dated Yiddish text is from the thirteenth century, although onomastic evidence for the language goes back to the end of the eleventh. See Marvin Herzog, "Yiddish," in *Jewish Languages*, ed. Paper, p. 47. Examples of Judeo-Spanish are even later still.

5. Regarding the many loanwords in old Arabic, particularly from Aramaic, see Siegmund Fraenkel, *Die aramäischen Fremdwörter im Arabischen* (1886; reprint, Hildesheim, 1962); and A. Jeffrey, *The Foreign Vocabulary of the Qur'ān* (Baroda, 1938). Many Aramaic words might also have come into Arabic from Christian sources.

6. See H. Z. [J. W.] Hirschberg, ed., *Der Diwan des as-Samaùal ibn 'Adijā'* (Krakow, 1931).

7. For the designations Proto-, Classical, and Modern Judeo-Arabic, see Norman A. Stillman, *Dictionary of the Middle Ages*, s.v. "Judeo-Arabic Language."

8. Moses b. Ezra, *Sēfer Shīrat Yisrā'ēl (Kitāb al-Muḥāḍara wa 'l-Mudhākara)*, Hebrew trans. B.-Z. Halper (reprint, Jerusalem, 1966–67), p. 53.

9. Judah al-Ḥarīzī, *Taḥkemōnī*, ed. Y. Toporovsky (Tel Aviv, 1952), p. 12.

10. This Andalusian pride in purity of lineage, language, and religious tradition is discussed in detail in Norman A. Stillman, "Aspects of Jewish Life in Islamic Spain," in *Aspects of Jewish Culture in the Middle Ages*, ed. Paul Szarmach (Albany, 1979), pp. 65–68; and more generally in idem, *The Jews of Arab Lands: A History and Source Book* (Philadelphia, 1979), p. 58.

11. The classic survey of medieval Judeo-Arabic literature is Moritz Steinschneider, *Die arabische Literatur der Juden* (Frankfurt a.M., 1902). Also valuable is the survey of Abraham S. Halkin, "Judeo-Arabic Literature," in *The Jews: Their History, Culture, and Religion*, ed. Louis Finkelstein, 3d ed. (New York, 1960), vol. 2, pp. 121–54.

12. Joshua Blau, *A Grammar of Mediaeval Judaeo-Arabic* (in Hebrew) (Jerusalem, 1961); and idem, *The Emergence and Linguistic Background of Judaeo-Arabic: A Study of the Origins of Middle Arabic* (Oxford, 1965).

13. Concerning this period, see Stillman, *Jews of Arab Lands*, pp. 64–94, and 255–323.

14. For examples of modern Iraqi Jewish writers of Arabic, see Shemuel Moreh, *Ḥibbūrē Yehūdīm ba-Sāfa hā-'Aravīt* (Jerusalem, 1973–74); and idem, "The Jewish Theater in Iraq in the First Half of the Twentieth Century" (in Hebrew), *Pe'amim* 23 (1985): 64—98.

15. Blau, *Grammar of Medieval Judaeo-Arabic*, p. 70, pars. 63–64; and idem, *Emergence and Linguistic Background of Judaeo-Arabic*, pp. 52–53, 58–61.

16. for /j/ > /z/ in the Geniza, see TS Box 28, f. 250, summarized by S. D. Goitein in *Tarbiz* 38 (1967): 26–27. Although there is a tendency among certain other groups (notably women, children, and some lower-class individuals) to make this substitution, it is nowhere as pronounced and as consistent as among Jews. Furthermore, as Brunot has pointed out, Muslim speakers know which /z/ in their speech corresponds to /j/ (or rather /ž/ in standard Muslim Moroccan Arabic), whereas "chez les israélites rien de semblable." See Louis Brunot, "Notes sur le parler arabe des Juifs de Fès," *Hespéris* 22:1 (1936): 10, par. 15. See also W. Marçais and H. Fleisch, *Encyclopaedia of Islam*, 2d ed., s.v. "Djīm."

17. TS NS J388, edited by S. D. Goitein in *Tarbiz* 38 (1967): 38–42; Antonin 904, edited by S. Assaf in *J. N. Epstein Jubilee Volume*, ed. S. Assaf et al. (Jerusalem, 1950), pp. 184–87.

18. TS NS 308, f. 119 (unedited), translated with notes by Norman A. Stillman in *International Journal of Middle East Studies* 5:2 (1974): 200–1.

19. A. S. Halkin, *Encyclopaedia Judaica* (1972), s.v. "Judaeo-Arabic Literature." A few voices did take issue with this long prevalent view. See, for example, S. D. Goitein, *Jews and Arabs*, pp. 199–205. See also the comments of Norman A. Stillman, "Response to Joshua Blau," in *Jewish Languages*, ed. Paper, p. 140.

20. For Yemen, see Nissim Gamlieli, *Ahavat Tēmān: ha-Shīra ha-'Amāmīt—Shīrat Nāshīm* (Tel Aviv, 1974–75); for Morocco, see Norman A. Stillman and Yedida K. Stillman, "The Art of a Moroccan Folk Poetess," *Zeitschrift der Deutschen Morgenländischen Gesellschaft* 128:1 (1978): 65–89; Joseph Chetrit, "Ha-Shīra ha-Īshīt veha-Ḥevrātīt be-'Aravīt-Yehūdīt shel Yehūdē Marōqō, in *Mi-Qedem ūmi-Yām: Meḥqārīm be-Yahadūt Arṣōt hā-Islām* (Haifa, 1981); for a sketch of Iraqi Judeo-Arabic folk literature that includes poetry, see Y. Avishur, "The Folk Literature of the Jews of Iraq in Judeo-Arabic" (in Hebrew), *Pe'amim* 3 (1979): 83–90.

21. Haïm Zafrani, *Etudes et recherches sur la vie intellectuelle juive au Maroc de la fin du 15e au debut du 20e siècle*, vol. 3, *Littératures dialectales et populaires juives en occident musulman: l'écrit et l'oral* (Paris, 1980).

22. Norman A. Stillman, *The Language and Culture of the Jews of Sefrou: An Ethno-Linguistic Study*. The Journal of Semitic Studies Monograph Series, no. 11 (Manchester, 1988).

23. For general introductions to the Maghrebi Arabic family, see Philippe

Marçais, *Esquisse grammaticale de l'Arabe Maghrébin* (Paris, 1977); and Alfred Willms, *Einführung in das Vulgärarabische von Nordwestafrika* (Leiden, 1972).

24. For an introductory linguistic breakdown of the varieties of Arabic spoken in Morocco, see G. S. Colin, "Les parlers: l'arabe," in *Initiation au Maroc*, 3d ed. (Paris, 1945), pp. 219–44. This basic dichotomy between pre-Hilālī sedentary forms of Arabic (urban and montagnard) and post-Hilālī Bedouin varieties was first distinguished by William Marçais. Marçais explains this fundamental linguistic split as being due to the two-stage arabization of North Africa: the first stage followed the initial conquests of the seventh century, and the second came in the aftermath of the Bedouin invasions of the eleventh century in the eastern Maghreb and the twelfth century in the western Maghreb. See William Marçais, *Articles et conférences* (Paris, 1961), pp. 171–92. Note should be taken here of Wexler's caution against the blanket assertions that all Jewish languages necessarily represent archaic forms of a cognate language. See Wexler, "Jewish Interlinguistics," *Language* 57:1 (1981): 102, n. 5.

25. For the language of the Fez mellah, see L. Brunot, "Notes sur le parler arabe des Juifs de Fès," pp. 1–32; L. Brunot and E. Malka, *Textes judéo-arabes de Fès* (Rabat, 1939); idem, *Glossaire judéo-arabe de Fès* (Rabat, 1940). For Rabat, see L. Brunot, *Textes arabes de Rabat*, vol. 1, *Textes, transcription, et traduction annotée* (Paris, 1931); idem, *Textes arabes de Rabat*, vol. 2, *Glossaire* (Paris, 1952). For Tetuan, see A. S. 'Abd al-'Āl, *Lahjat Shamāl al-Maghrib: Tiṭwān wa-mā Ḥawluhā* (Cairo, 1968); and idem, *Mu'jam Shamāl al-Maghrib* (Cairo, 1968).

26. For descriptive studies of Jebli dialects, see George S. Colin, "Notes sur le parler arabe du nord de la région de Taza," *Bulletin de l'Institut Française d'Archéologie Orientale* 18:1 (1921): 33–119; and E. Lévi-Provençal, *Textes arabes de l'Ouargha Dialecte des Jbala (Maroc Septentrional)* (Paris, 1922). See also 'Abd al-'Āl's *Lahjat Shamāl al-Maghrib* and *Mu'jam Shamāl al-Maghrib*, which cover both the urban speech of Tetuan and the Jebli dialects that surround it.

27. Louis Brunot, *Introduction à l'arabe marocain* (Paris, 1950), p. 18. On the other hand, Brunot does, however, recognize the fact that there are important differences even between Jewish varieties (he prefers to call them "dialects") of Arabic, noting: "Il faut ajouter que le dialecte arabe des juifs de Rabat est nettement different de celui des juifs de Salé, Fès, Sefrou, etc. . . ; chaque Mellah a, peut-on dire, son parler original" (Brunot, *Texte arabes de Rabat*, vol. 1, p. xv).

28. Joseph Chetrit, "Niveaux, registres de langues et sociolectes dans les langues judéo-arabes du Maroc," in *Les relations entre Juifs et Musulmans en Afrique du Nord, XIX*e*—XX*e *siècles* (Paris, 1980), p. 130.

29. Ibid., p. 130. Birnbaum makes a similar argument in his "Jewish Language," in *Essays in Honour of the Very Rev. Dr. J. H. Hertz*, pp. 64–65.

30. Brunot and Malka, *Glossaire judéo-arabe de Fès*, p. 121. Not having a specific name for a language, even among its own speakers, is not a rare phenomenon in Jewish and general linguistic history. Hebrew is only referred to as "the language of Canaan" in the Bible (Isa. 19:18) and as "Judean" (2

Kings 18:26). Yiddish for much of its history was only called *Taytsh* (cf. German *Deutsch*) and *Loshn Ashkenaz* ("the language of Ashkenaz). This indicates only that for a long period Jews were aware of "a proximity of their language to German, but that they had no particular interests in stressing the uniqueness of their language by means of the name" (Weinreich, *History of the Yiddish Language*, p. 315).

31. See note 2 above.

32. Haim Blanc, *Communal Dialects in Baghdad* (Cambridge, Mass., 1964), p. 15, sec. 2.23. However note Wexler's caution against taking this approach so far:

> Jewish languages could also be compared with so-called "confessional," "professional," and "communal" dialects; but suggestions to define Jewish languages as confessional variants of a non-Jewish language are ill-conceived.
> (Wexler, "Jewish Interlinguistics," p. 136.)

33. The same cultural argument for this approach has been made by Paper in his introduction to *Jewish Languages: Theme and Variations*, ed. Paper, p. vii. It is also a central theme in Birnbaum, "Jewish Languages," in *Essays in Honour of the Very Rev. Dr. J. H. Hertz*, pp. 51–67; and again in condensed form in idem, *Encyclopaedia Judaica* (1972), s.v. "Jewish Languages."

34. Cf. Muslim *aš-qal-lek.*

35. Cf. Muslim *ăs-axbarkum.*

36. Cf. Muslim *ha huwa žay.*

37. Thus, in Sefriwi Judeo-Arabic /kţebţ/ means both "I wrote" and "you wrote" (cf. Muslim /kţebţ/, /kţebţi/) and/ţekţeb/ means both "you" (m.s.) and "you (f.s.) write" (cf. Muslim /ţekţeb/, /ţekţebi/).

38. The use of two different verbs for "to pass away" reflect different religious and cultural models. /Nifṭār/ is from Rabbinic Hebrew literature, while /teweffa/ is Koranic.

39. The word /keswa/ is only used in Judeo-Arabic in the form /l-keswa l-kebira/, which designates the Andalusian wedding dress worn by Jewish women in the cities of the north and the coastal regions. See Yedida K. Stillman, "The Costume of the Jewish Woman in Morocco," in *Studies in Jewish Folklore*, ed. Frank Talmage (Cambridge, Mass., 1980), pp. 349–52.

40. The Judeo-Arabic words are derived from the nominative and the Muslim Arabic words from the accusative in the Classical language.

41. Ze'ev Chomsky, *ha-Lāshōn ha-'Ivrīt be-Darkhē Hitpatḥūtāh* (Jerusalem, 1967), p. 17. Herbert H. Paper, however, cautions against the accuracy and value of such word counts (oral communications).

42. Goitein, *Jews and Arabs*, p. 133.

43. Moshe Bar-Asher, "Al ha-Yesōdōt ha-'Ivriyyīm ba-'Aravīt ha-Medubberet shel Yehūdē Marōqō," *Leshonenu* 42:3–4 (1978): p. 166, par. 6, and p. 168, par. 10.

44. Eccles. 5:6

Trade as a Mediator in Muslim–Jewish Relations: Southwestern Morocco in the Nineteenth Century[1]

Daniel Schroeter

OF ALL the countries of the Arab world, nowhere were Jews more numerous than in Morocco. And with the exception of Poland, there was perhaps no other part of the world where Jews were so ubiquitous in both town and countryside. In most parts of Morocco, Jews were to be found in the urban bazaar and the weekly and seasonal rural markets. It was in the marketplace above all where Jews and Muslims interacted. Trade, therefore, served as a mediator between them. This dimension has been frequently discussed by anthropologists.[2] But it has not been examined in depth by historians, who have been limited by the question of whether or not Muslim-Jewish relations were good or bad, and the degree to which the Jewish position improved or deteriorated as foreign intervention grew in the nineteenth century. Out of these interrelated questions, there appear to be two principal positions: (1) that relations between Jews and Muslims were essentially good until foreign intervention disturbed the harmony[3] and (2) that Muslim-Jewish relations were generally poor, though pressures from the foreign powers led to an improvement in Jewish status.[4]

The status of Jews in Morocco fluctuated in relationship to political and economic changes, especially as foreign interference grew in the nineteenth century. But this did not necessarily disrupt the structure of Muslim-Jewish relations as they functioned on a day-to-day basis. Foreign inroads paradoxically both heightened intercommunal tensions and strengthened interdependencies between Muslims and Jews.

Tensions were increased because a relatively large number of Jews were associated with the foreign powers. At the same time, the boost in commerce with Europe led to the formation of new Jewish communities and the construction of new socioeconomic ties. These symbiotic economic ties defined the nature of Muslim-Jewish relations in the marketplace well into the twentieth century. This does not suggest an absence of the kind of intercommunal tensions inherent in majority-minority relationships that are frequently exacerbated by colonialism. Both the social boundaries and the inferior legal status of Jews in Muslim society implied mutual suspicion and contempt. As a minority group, Jews were manipulated, but they were also able to take advantage of opportunities presented by the foreign powers in Morocco. But trade and the marketplace remained the chief mediator in minimizing intercommunal tensions.

Ethnic Spatial Boundaries

In most urban settings in nineteenth-century Morocco, the Jewish communities were confined to specifically designated residential quarters known as mellahs (literary *millāḥ*). Jews from early times tended to group together in close proximity, but it was between the fifteenth and nineteenth centuries that mellahs were constructed in many Moroccan cities, with Jews forced to live in them.[5] The reasons for the establishment of exclusive Jewish quarters are attributed to the desire of the sultan either to protect the Jews or to ostracize them—aims that need not have been incompatible. This can be better understood if the question of mellahs is analyzed in the context of the city as a whole and in terms of town-country relations.

The Jewish urban population of Morocco was undoubtedly augmented by the influx of Spanish and Portuguese Jews in the fifteenth and sixteenth centuries. As the only non-Muslim religious minority in Morocco, the Jews therefore had special communal needs. Since it was considered both undesirable and inappropriate for Jews to expand their social and religious space within the proximity of the mosques,[6] the construction of mellahs could serve the purposes of segregating Jewish social activity from the Muslims and of administering and/or protecting the community as a definable spatial unit.[7] During times of rural unrest, urban Jews were vulnerable to attack and this challenged the authority of the government. It was considered more practical for the government to *protect* the Jews within the walled confines of the mellah. Indeed, the whole governmental ideology of Muslim-Jewish relations was based on a protégé pact system *(dhimma)*. Attacks against Jews *(ahl adh-dhimma)* violated the sacrosanctity *(ḥurma)* promised by the pact.

This dual system of protection and confinement was reproduced in areas outside the control of the sultan. Mellahs existed in various villages and small towns in southwestern Morocco, and they had a similar spatial relationship to the rest of the settlement as in the makhzan towns (seats of government and administration).[8] Here as well, it was the function of the local leader to assure the protection of the *dhimmī*.

A distinctive feature of Muslim cities generally was the division between a well-ordered, open part of the city and a sector predominated by a web of narrow alleyways. It has been shown that this division was based on a fundamental differentiation between the "public city," dominated by large-scale economic activity, and the "private city," where family life was relatively segregated. This typical Mediterranean division was clearly perceived and formulated by Muslim jurists.[9] Within this structure, Jewish residential quarters had to be separate so that the private world of Jewish family life and religion could be freely expressed. Yet on a business level Jews interacted with Muslims in the wide open spaces of the urban market. With nightfall, or in the event that the public part of the city was being used for a Muslim celebration, Jews receded into their private sector, the mellah. There was a conscious understanding between Jew and Muslim regarding these boundaries: neither penetrated into the other's private sector, but both were free to trade and even interact socially in the business sector. This system was only disrupted in times of urban disorders or rural rebellion.

This general model can be seen in the makhzan-controlled southwestern seaport of Essaouira in the nineteenth century. Essaouira had a Jewish population that ranged between 30 and 50 percent of the population. The mellah of Essaouira comprised between an eighth and a ninth of the area of the town[10] (see figure 1). Initially the Jews did not live in a separate quarter, but in 1807, a mellah was established by Sultan Sulaymān as part of a wider policy of confining the Jews of several coastal towns to well-defined quarters (walled-in Jewish quarters had already existed in the imperial cities of Fez, Marrakesh, and Meknes for a few centuries).[11] The mellah of Essaouira was constructed in the far northeastern corner of the town. Only the wealthy royal trading Jews, who had a special status, were allowed to reside in the official casbah quarter, on the opposite end of town. In the latter half of the nineteenth century, the Jewish population of Essaouira doubled, and the city's mellah became extremely squalid and overcrowded. Unable to expand outside the confines of the mellah, the residential buildings spiraled upward, much as in the ghettos of Europe. Government regulations prohibiting the construction of third stories were disregarded by Jewish speculators, as conditions of overcrowding intensified in the 1890s.[12]

Figure 1: Essaouira

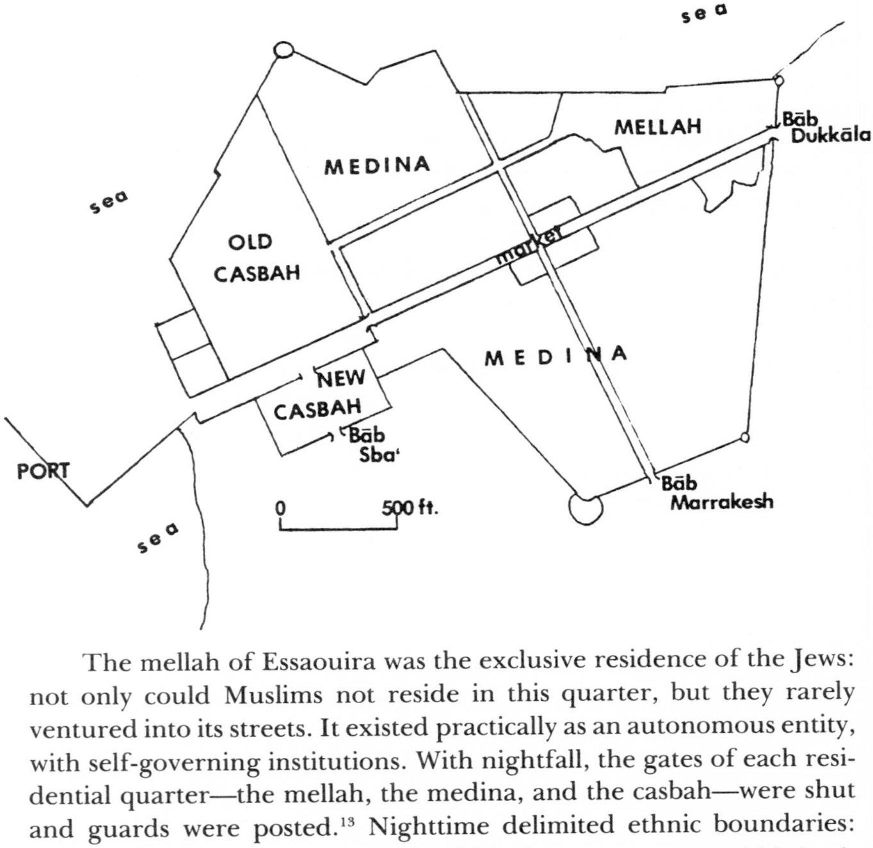

The mellah of Essaouira was the exclusive residence of the Jews: not only could Muslims not reside in this quarter, but they rarely ventured into its streets. It existed practically as an autonomous entity, with self-governing institutions. With nightfall, the gates of each residential quarter—the mellah, the medina, and the casbah—were shut and guards were posted.[13] Nighttime delimited ethnic boundaries: During the day, the Jew maintained his shops or conducted his business in the markets of the medina. After nightfall, the Jew found security among his coreligionists, behind the closed and guarded gates of the mellah—in a sense moving from the profane activities of the market to the sacred Jewish world of the mellah.[14] In contrast to the Muslims whose central mosque *(jāmi')* was situated on the main thoroughfare of the bazaar, all the Jewish synagogues were located in the mellah (except for those of the wealthy, which were in the casbah quarter). It was within the confines of the Jewish quarter, for example, that the kabbalists would meet for nocturnal sessions, which sometimes continued until dawn.[15] The social and religious world of the Jews was an alien and forbidden place—*terra incognita*—for the Muslims.

The same kind of spatial relations were found in the small mellahs of southwestern Morocco. In the case of Iligh of the Anti-Atlas, the mellah was situated in the far northeastern section of the village, separated from the residence of the nobles (colloquial *shurfa*; literary *sharif*; pl. *shurafā'*) by the slave quarters. Though the Jews of Iligh lived in a Berber-speaking region (the Tashelḥit dialect of southwestern Morocco), the language of the mellah (called lashūniya) was an Arabic that, except for a few characteristic Jewish inflections and lexical deviations,[16] was spoken by Muslim city dwellers in other parts of Morocco. But as it was a language not well understood by most of the Muslim Berber population, the Jewish men therefore all spoke fluent Tashelḥit, which was indispensable for commercial dealings. The majority of the Jews of Iligh were peddlers or itinerant traders who were involved in both the trade of the local markets as well as the long-distance and trans-Saharan trade. Ethnic boundaries were defined then not only by social and religious space, but by linguistic space as well.

Jews in Urban and Rural Markets

In the urban markets, ethnic barriers were broken down. Jewish traders were subject to the same administration as were their Muslim counterparts. In the town of Essaouira, Jewish commercial activities in the bazaar came under the surveillance of the *muḥtasib* just as did Muslim activities. Jews were free to rent shops from the *habous* (literary *ḥubus*; pl. *aḥbās*), the Muslim religious endowments.[17] The requirements of business overrode religious differences.

So dominant was the Jewish presence in the urban markets of Essaouira, that on Saturdays, the bustling bazaar area of town came to a virtual standstill.[18] Already on Friday afternoons, the Jews of the town flocked to the cemetery in supplication to their saints *(ṣaddīqīm)*.[19]

From sunset on Friday evening and throughout Saturday, the markets of the town were virtually empty. Itinerant Jewish peddlers as well, who during the week plied their wares in the rural markets, returned to their families in the mellah for the Jewish Sabbath.

The market relationship of town and country depended on a string of weekly rural markets. It was above all Jewish peddlers who brought urban goods to the countryside and rural products to the city. They were also an essential link between the cities and distant markets. The result was an interdependent relationship between Muslim and Jew, and a social and juridical web of patron-client relations, which assured, under most circumstances, the neutrality of trade routes and marketplaces.[20]

The vast majority of the Jewish population of Essaouira was engaged in some kind of activity connected to trade. At the beginning of the twentieth century, when the Alliance Israélite Universelle began to count the Jewish population, the director of the Alliance school noted that "out of a population of 10,000 souls one would only find 150 families who live from practicing their trades; the remainder include merchants, peddlers and hucksters."[21] The Alliance census of the Jewish population in 1913 revealed that 60 percent of the working population was involved in some form of commerce.[22] In Jewish communities in some of the smaller towns and villages in the Sous, virtually the entire male population were itinerant traders and peddlers. Such was the case in the town of Iligh.

From the town of Essaouira, peddlers and itinerant traders served as agents of the wholesale merchants, distributing European imports such as textiles, tea, and sugar to markets both near and far. In exchange for goods or specie, they obtained almonds, olive oil, goatskins, gum sandarac, and other items of Haha and the Sous, which they brought to town for export. Often the itinerant peddler was a small merchant in his own right and would buy goods in one rural market and sell at a profit in another. Some plied the weekly markets, returning to the town on Sabbath; others left for protracted stays at much more distant markets, returning twice a year, for Passover and the New Year.[23]

The Jewish predominance in trade is reflected in both weekly and seasonal market cycles. Weekly trade rhythms in town revolved around the Jewish Sabbath. This can be determined by examining a register of gate and market taxes for the year A.H. 1301 (1883–84)[24]

Figure 2. Gate and Market Taxes in Essaouira: Averages by Day of the Week (1301/1883–84)

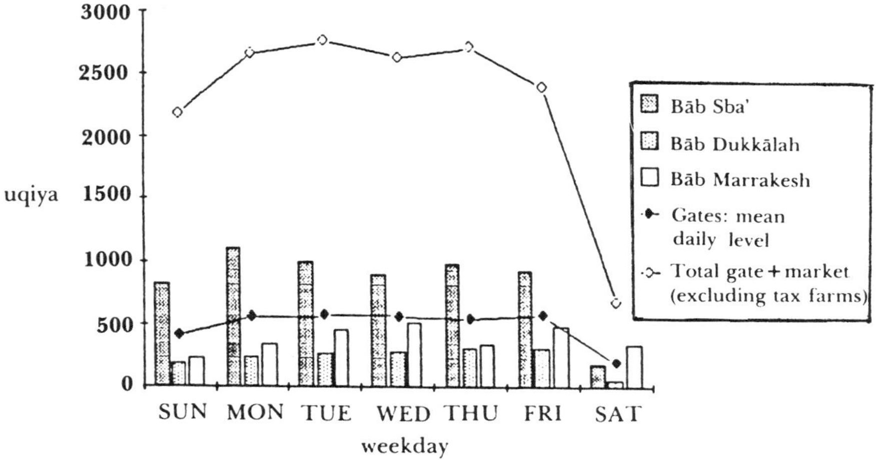

(see figure 2). The overall revenue from the gates and markets of the town dropped dramatically on Saturdays. Traffic through Bāb Sbaʿ, the gateway to the south, dropped significantly on the Sabbath. Bāb Dukkālah, contiguous to the mellah, had practically no traffic on Saturdays. Bāb Marrakesh, passing through Muslim residential areas and most distant from the bazaar, had the most traffic on the Jewish Sabbath. Activity on Sunday was also well below average. It seems probable that many Jewish ambulent traders left town following the Sabbath, with few returning through the gates the same day, as is shown by the lower tax revenues for Sundays. More traffic passed through the gates on Fridays than on any other weekday, an indicator that the itinerant Jewish peddler returned home to celebrate the Sabbath with his family.

Revenue is another index of market activity. Trade was clearly slower in all the markets on Saturdays, since little revenue accrued from the markets on that day. Some sectors in the market were clearly monopolized by the Jews (see figure 3). No taxes at all were taken from the edible oil market *(al-qaʿa)* and the cobblers' leather market *(aṭ-ṭarrāf)* on Saturdays. The goatskin market of Essaouira, probably the largest in Morocco, was dominated by Jews. There was only one Saturday during the entire year of 1301 that revenue was recorded (and that was probably an error on the part of the record keeper).

Thursday was the busiest day of the week for the meat and slaughterhouse market, preceding both the big Muslim *jum'a* meal on Friday afternoons and the festive Sabbath meal on Friday evenings.

Figure 3. Average Revenues by Day of the Week for Various Markets in Essaouira (1301/1883–84)

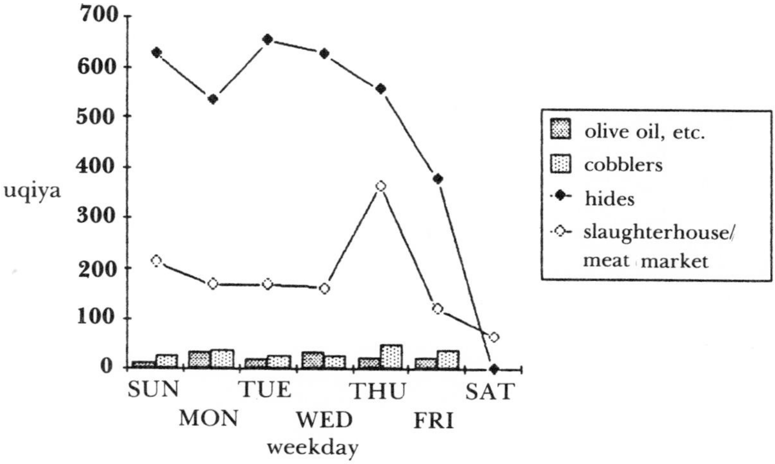

Muslim and Jewish Festivals

Seasonal market cycles depended on the convergence of Muslim and Jewish festivals. The two periods of Jewish festivals that most markedly influenced economic life were the time of the Passover, falling between the end of March and the end of April, and the three autumn festivals of Rosh Hashanah, Yom Kippur, and Sukkoth, falling between the beginning of September and mid-October. These Jewish festivals fall at the beginning and the end of the period for the majority of Muslim "popular" religious pilgrimages of southwestern Morocco, known as *moussems* (literary *mawsim*; pl. *mawāsim*; Tashelḥit *amūggars*). Unlike the universal Muslim "orthodox" festivals, which revolve around the lunar year, the *moussems* fall about the same date each season, following the Julian cadendar. In fact, the Julian months are used in the vernacular nomenclature.[25] Both Jews and Muslims organized their commercial time around the requirements of these celebrations.[26]

The Jewish itinerant traders of Essaouira would often head south after Passover, only to return home for the Jewish New Year in the autumn. Furthermore, the *moussems* were often the scene of intense trading activities. The *shurfa* of Iligh in Tazerwalt, the heirs of the marabout (literary *murābiṭ*) Sī Ḥmad ū Mūsā (Sīdī Aḥmad ū Mūsā), capitalized on the arrival of large numbers of pilgrims at the shrine of the saint and in the mid-nineteenth century turned the *moussem* into the most important biannual emporium of southern Morocco. Caravans from all over southern Morocco, the Sahara, and Timbuktu converged twice a year on the village in which the shrine of the marabout was located, at the end of March and at the end of August or beginning of September.[27] Since Jewish traders were not allowed to reside in or enter the village, an encampment on the outskirts of the village was consigned to them during the time of *moussem*.[28] However, many Jews did live in Iligh, the place of residence of the Bū Damī'a family—the descendants of the marabout. Indeed the Jewish community of Iligh was crucial for the economic strength of the *shurfa*, linking together most of southwestern Morocco through their ties to Jewish traders in other communities.[29]

The convergence of the Jewish festivals of the spring and autumn, the *moussems*, and the harvest season governed the ebb and flow of commercial activity in the town of Essaouira. Traffic through the southern gate, Bāb Sba', reached its annual peak in 1884 just before Passover. Total market revenue surged to its highest point during the Jewish New Year season. During the days leading up to Rosh Hashanah and the following festivals, Yom Kippur and Sukkoth, activity in the town reached a frenzy. In 1884, the week of Yom Kippur and Sukkoth converged with the biggest orthodox Muslim festival, 'Īd al-Aḍḥā, in the Muslim month of Dhū al-Ḥijja. This clearly greatly increased commercial activity, which is reflected in the gate and market tax register (see figure 4). In the preceding month of Dhū al-Qa'da, more revenue was collected than during any other month of the year.

What can be tentatively reconstructed from the fluctuations of revenue collected from gates and markets during these weeks of 1884? Clearly Muslims were profiting from the Jewish festivals by furnishing Jews with needed commodities. Muslim commercial activity even spilled over into the day of Rosh Hashanah, which was also a Sabbath that year *(yōm shabbat we-yōm ṭōb)*, a day in which no Jew would have been found in the markets. Trading during the ten days leading up to Yom Kippur, followed two days later by 'Īd al-Aḍḥā, fluctuated dramatically. On the second day of the New Year, still celebrated by the Jews, little activity appeared in the *sūq*s of the town, but the following day there was a sudden upsurge. During the next ten days the market was jolted by dramatic fluctuations, as determined by the Sabbath and the approach of the festivals. Then, on ʿĪd al-Aḍḥā, much like a Jewish Sabbath in Essaouira, there was virtually no commerce. Finally after Sukkoth, which fell on 13 Dhū al-Ḥijja, fluctuations became much more regular.

The evidence therefore demonstrates what has been observed elsewhere in Morocco: the Jewish peddler might be absent for most of the year—returning home to his family to celebrate Rosh Hashanah and Yom Kippur, then leaving again just after Sukkoth, and returning only for Passover in the spring.[30] In Essaouira, therefore, it was in September that trading activity reached its height. Rosh Hashanah followed the annual fair of Sī Ḥmad ū Mūsā and the arrival of one of the three annual trans-Saharan caravans, all contributing to this rhythm.[31]

Patrons and Clients

This interdependent system of Jewish and Muslim religious and commercial time would only work because of another kind of crucial relationship—that of patron and client. The Jewish merchants of Essaouira were protected by the sultan, who originally gave them the official authorization to engage in foreign trade. These "court Jews" were tied to the sultan in a contractual relationship of credit and debt. The Palace granted interest-free loans and sometimes credit on customs duties to the merchants *(tujjār as-Sulṭān)* to help them establish their businesses. These debts owed the Palace were then repaid in monthly installments from the profits accruing from trade. Interest was forbidden by Islam, but the Palace was able to profit indirectly from the loans by the customs duties that the merchants had to pay to the port.[32]

Once this relationship between *tājir* and sultan was established, the former could move to another town or travel abroad only after receiving authorization from the sultan himself. This was only granted after the *tājir* left a guarantor *(ḍāmin)* and deposited money or property as collateral *(rahn)*.[33] Yet conversely, the sultan was obligated to protect the Jew's goods along the trade routes and to aid him in the

Figure 4. Gate and Market Taxes in Essaouira during the Jewish New Year Period (5645/1301/1884)

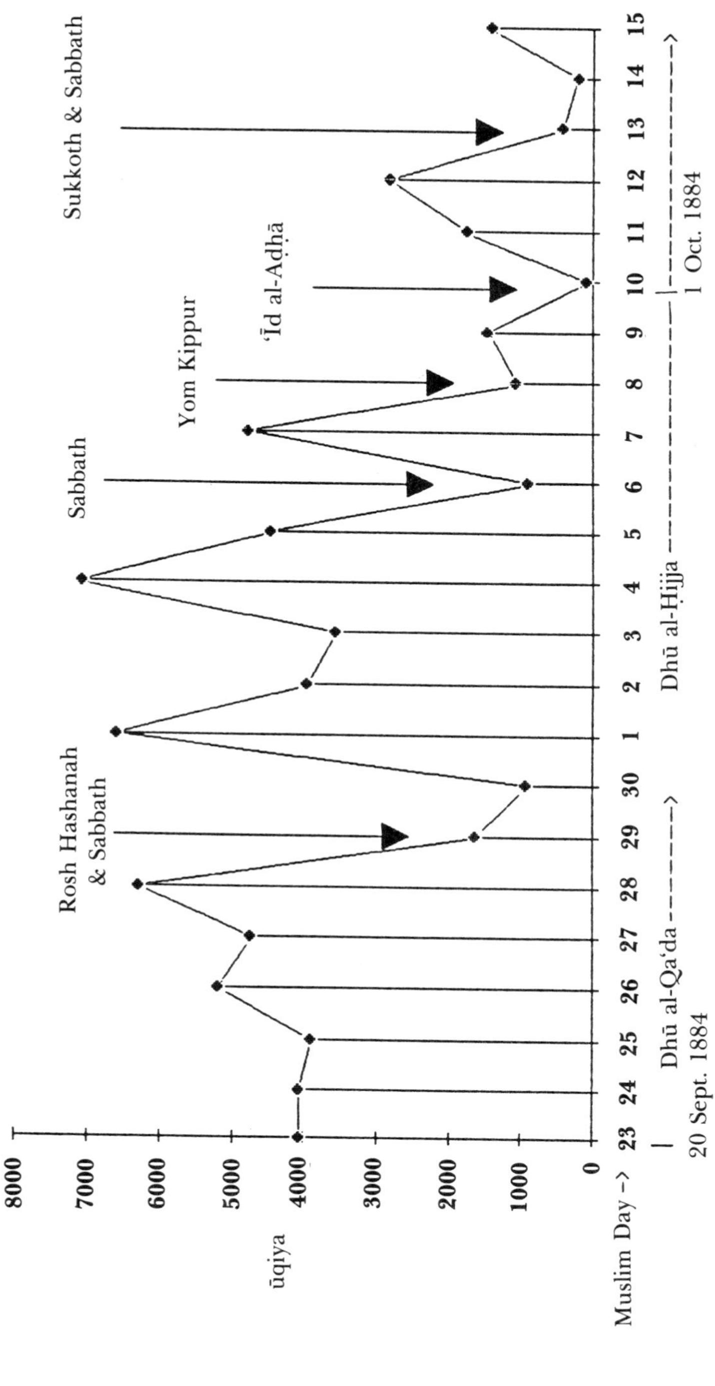

recovery of debts. In 1846, for example, a caid instructs Ḥusayn ū Hāshim, the marabout of Iligh, that a Jewish *tājir* of the sultan, Sāhūl (Saul), has been sent to recover debts owed him by Jews and Muslims of Iligh and Ifrane. The sultan has written to the caid to assist the Jew, and the caid now asks the sharif to help because "his money has now become the money of the sultan (may he be victorious)." As the caid explains, "The Jew is one of the merchants of the sultan, *and must be protected,* both out of respect for the sacrosanctity of the sultan and for the sacrosanctity of the protégés *(ahl adh-dhimma)*, since the Prophet (God bless him and grant him salvation) granted their protection."[34]

For travel, the central government was only able to assure safety in limited areas. Radiating out from the makhzan-controlled town of Essaouira were officially protected stations, called *nazāla*s, which sheltered the itinerant traders at night for a small fee levied on beasts, loads of merchandise, and Jews. Occasionally lodgers were attacked in these government stations. Therefore, some traders regarded the *nazāla*s as an obstacle and tried to avoid them by camping out at night. But for the most part, it was in the interests of the makhzan to protect the trade routes connecting the capital of Marrakesh with the royal seaport of Essaouira.[35]

Most of the caravans and traders in southwestern Morocco had to pass through areas outside the direct control of the central government. In these regions, the sultan could offer little protection. Traders, therefore, needed the assurance of safe passage through distant and potentially treacherous regions in which they operated. Jews often were compelled to pay tribute to the tribesmen who ruled the regions that they crossed. A kind of passage toll called *zaṯṯāṯa* (Berber, "a small piece of cloth"; symbolically some kind of fabric was probably exchanged) was required by those guaranteeing safe passage *(zaṯṯāṯ)*.[36]

It was through a network of patron-client relations that the Jews were generally able to travel unmolested through southwestern Morocco. A relationship was generally established between Muslim and Jew by *dhabīḥa*, a ritual slaughter of a sheep or bull by the Jew before a Berber or Arab patron (the *sīd*) of power and influence who could assure his client's protection. The sacrifice formed a bond called *mezrag* (Berber, "spear,")[37] or alternatively *al-'ār* (Arabic, "shame").[38] Henceforth the client was under the protection of his patron or, for that matter, of the whole tribe. Annual payments in linen or sugar would be made subsequently to the chief. These pacts were inherited jointly by the offspring of both patron and client and were in fact rigorously maintained. The relationship facilitated travel and commerce since the Jew was subsequently protected by his patron: an attack against the Jew was regarded as a violation against the chief or tribe assuring the protection, and violent retribution was considered legitimate.[39]

The most powerful patrons of all were the marabouts of the southern *zāwiya*s (literally "corner"; the term *zāwiya* refers to a religious confraternity), whose fortunes were derived from their control of the trade routes. They, like the sultan, sought to protect the merchants who formed the basis of their political and economic power. Shaykh Abū Bakr of the Nāṣiriyya *zāwiya* of Tamgrout in the Dra‘ protected caravans and Swiri merchants involved in the trans-Saharan trade. The itinerant traders traveling to the *moussem* of Sī Ḥmad ū Mūsā were assured protection all along the trade route by the marabout and the saint's descendant, Ḥusayn ū Hāshim of Iligh. When brigandage was rife, the marabout assured repayment to the pillaged trader. At the *moussem* Ḥusayn would seize goods belonging to the people from the territory in which the robbery had taken place.[40] The marabouts, like the sultan, extended the *ḥurma* of their *zāwiya*s along the trade routes traveled by *their* Jews.

In those areas not directly under the sultan's authority, the relationship between patron and client—*sīd* and *dhimmī*—constituted a reproduction, mutatis mutandis, of the same kind of relationship that existed betwen sultan and Jew.[41] The stereotypical portrayal of Berber-Jewish relations suggests that the position of the rural Jew of the Atlas and the Anti-Atlas was much better than in the makhzan-controlled cities.[42] Much of this has to do with the colonial image of two antagonistic realms, the *bled makhzen* and *bled siba*—the region under the control of the sultan and dissident regions—a dichotomy that colonial historiography generally breaks down between Arab and Berber.[43] The position and security of the Jew, in fact, depended on other circumstances and might have nothing to do with whether or not the sultan's authority extended over a particular area. One factor was whether the area was urban or rural. Another crucial factor was the degree to which order could be maintained. The security of the Jew, whether in an urban or rural, Arab or Berber setting, was jeopardized during times of unrest.

But as a generalization, the evidence seems to suggest that a similar kind of relationship prevailed between *sīd* and Jew in the Anti-Atlas, and sultan and Jew in makhzan-controlled areas. In both cases, the Jewish merchant and itinerant trader lived a kind of quasi-feudal existence, in which his fiscal obligations to his lord and protector restricted his freedom of movement. Once authorized to trade for his *sīd* or sultan, the Jew was compelled to maintain his residence under his master's protection. In Iligh, virtually the entire male population was involved in trade; the mellah itself was the personal possession of the sharif. No Jew was allowed to leave without the chief's authorization.[44] With the economic eclipse of Iligh in the years following the death of Ḥusayn ū Hāshim, some Jews began to regard their residence at Iligh as bondage. A contemporary in Essaouira reports:

> The Jews living in the province of Sous live in security, sitting peacefully under vine and fig tree, living tranquilly with their ruling masters, and conducting their commerce in fraternity and friendship with the natives. But under the rule of one chief, named Sīdī Muḥammad b. Sīdī al-Ḥusayn ū Hās[h]im, the fate of the poor Jews is bad and bitter, for they are in dire straits: they are denied justice in the law, both person and possession belong to their master whose terror frightens them, and they tremble before his voice. He does not know the way of peace, there is no justice in his realm and he follows his heart's whim. Most of his army and servants who follow his orders are his black slaves; he does not even finish talking and the ones opposing him fall by the hand of the sons of Ham . . . . The Jews cannot go out from his province to settle in a neighboring province for he does not allow them and their families to leave; the men go out with their merchandise but their wives and children remain as hostages.[45]

At the same time, the sharif assures that the Jews belonging to *his* mellah are not violated, and he might even intervene to protect the Jews living in the mellah of a rival.[46]

The influential Jewish *tujjār as-Sulṭān* were also powerful patrons themselves. Throughout the interior of Morocco, the Jewish merchants of Essaouira maintained a string of Jewish commission agents, who sold import items or exchanged them for export commodities. Often the agents were tied to the *tujjār* by a commenda agreement *(qirāḍ)*. In this form of contract, the merchant provided the capital, though the profits were divided equally between the two parties. In the event of an honest loss, the agent owed nothing to the supplier of the sum.[47] In southern Morocco, it was often the case that the itinerant trader was simultaneously tied to the Jewish merchant houses in Essaouira and to the powerful Muslim chiefs such as Ḥusayn ū Hāshim or Shaykh Bayrūk of Goulimine.[48]

Muslim merchants as well often depended on Jewish brokers to market their merchandise in the countryside or in other inland cities.[49] Jews relied on Muslim transporters and caravans to convey their goods over long distances. The wealthy Jewish town merchants of Essaouira, such as Corcos and Elmaleh, often advanced interest-free loans *(salaf)* to the rural chiefs without stipulating when the loan should be returned.[50] Personal ties and trust between rural leaders and the Jewish merchants were crucial for the smooth operation of exchange. While the chiefs relied on the Jews for advances in capital, the Jews needed the assurance of the free circulation of goods and, when the need arose, of aid to recover debts.[51] The rural chiefs assured protection to the Jewish *tujjār*: when Essaouira was pillaged by the tribes following the bombardment by the French, some of the leading Jews found refuge among the Berber chiefs to the south of the town.[52]

During the course of the nineteenth century, the Jewish merchants often acquired foreign consular protection or became consular representatives of foreign powers themselves, enabling them therefore to provide protection to the rural Muslims. Abraham Corcos and his son Meyer, wealthy Jewish merchants who both served as American vice-consul, were tied to rural Muslims by the oath, *al-'ār*. Meyer Corcos reports on this state of affairs:

> As a custom in Morocco, it is wrong to turn out of the house people who bring such sign of refuge called *El Aar*. My late father has many times, and for many months Moors lodging in the house whom he could not send away until they chose to go themselves, and several times my late father settled amicably affairs pending between his lodgers and the governors of the surrounding districts.[53]

Here the Muslim-patron—Jew-client model is reversed. The powerful Jewish merchants of Essaouira were able to extend protection to Muslims, mirroring the marabouts of the south. Merchant houses became sanctuaries, just like the *zāwiya*s.

The Expansion of Jewish Trading Networks

These interdependencies between Muslim and Jew continued to develop and expand during the nineteenth century. As foreign economic penetration grew, new trade networks were established. The importation of foreign goods at the port of Essaouira expanded exchanges in southwestern Morocco and spurred the development of a number of Jewish communities along the trade routes. The overall Jewish population of Morocco may have dropped during this period because of recurrent droughts and epidemics. But while some Jewish communities declined, others developed at the new centers of distribution of European commodities. Jews in Essaouira, through their agents in the southwest, became the principal distributors of the main import commodities: textiles, tea, and sugar.

Jewish traders were also instrumental in the export trade. In the early nineteenth century, the Jewish community of Goulimine witnessed a tremendous growth, the result of the domination of the Saharan and trans-Saharan trade by the Shaykh Bayrūk.[54] The Afriat family of Goulimine established itself in Essaouira and rapidly made a fortune in the gum export trade.[55] By the mid-nineteenth century, Iligh under the rule of Ḥusayn ū Hāshim became the major center of power. By fostering the commercial development of the *moussem*, the Jewish community of Iligh grew into an important trading community, specializing in trade in ostrich feathers,[56] then in demand in Victorian England owing to a fashion in plumed hats.

As new distribution networks opened up, intermediary trading communities developed along the routes. Iligh grew rapidly due to the expansion of the trade of Essaouria. The ancient Jewish community of Ifrane to the south of Iligh, virtually destroyed in a rebellion of Bū Iḥlās about 1790–92, was revitalized by the development of the *moussem*.[57] As Essaouira's trade began to expand, new mellahs were established near Imi n'Tanaoute, southwest of Essaouira in the foothills of the Atlas Mountains.[58] At the end of the nineteenth century, when Essaouira lost much of its importance in international commerce, the town began to rely more on local trade. It is probable that several new Jewish communities cropped up in Essaouira's hinterland. Jewish pilgrimage *(hillūla)* to the tomb of Rabbi Nessim b. Nessim at Aït Bayoud was born in the last decades of the nineteenth century. Commercial exchange with the Muslim population was combined with the visit to the *ṣaddīq*.[59]

Foreign Intervention and Muslim-Jewish Tensions

It is clear that interdependencies grew as foreign economic penetration expanded Morocco's commercial exchange. This did not, however, prevent growing tensions in some areas between Muslims and Jews. The system of foreign protection gave some Jews extraterritorial rights, enabling them to evade the specific stipulations of the *dhimma* pact. This certainly constituted a challenge to the system, and it became a major concern of the makhzan.[60] Furthermore, as foreign interference grew, the Moroccan government's capacity to rule decreased. The makhzan was increasingly unable to assure stability, even in the areas it controlled. From 1868 through 1873, the Haha region was in constant rebellion, at times threatening the security of the town of Essaouira itself.[61] Incessant outbreaks of violence and brigandage characterized the decades leading up to the establishment of the French protectorate in 1912.

Undoubtedly, the Jewish itinerant peddler was vulnerable to attack, and both the Alliance Israélite Universelle and the Anglo-Jewish Association lobbied the foreign consulates to intervene whenever a Jewish peddler was killed. The robbery and murder of peddlers in the countryside, however, was probably not directed exclusively at Jews (although there are no records about non-Jewish victims during this period). Even if more Jews than non-Jews were killed by brigands, it was probably because of the higher proportion of Jewish peddlers who carried money and merchandise into the countryside.[62]

There are indications that the growth in foreign penetration in Morocco increased tensions between Muslims and Jews. Many Jewish itinerant traders became protégés of foreign powers, and when they were agents of Muslim merchants, this could lead to complicated disputes between the makhzan and the foreign consulates. Furthermore, the government adopted administrative reforms when it was alleged that protégés of foreign merchant firms were claiming substantial losses from theft. It was decreed by the central government that four notaries *('udūl)* were to register all goods and money of Jewish peddlers before the latter left the towns.[63] The system of protection in the second half of the nineteenth century led to all kinds of difficulties that strained relations between Jews and the authorities. For example, protégés were not subject to the gate and market taxes. As a consequence, goods were often consigend to protégés to evade the octroi.[64] Ironically, it was often Jewish protégés who were the tax farmers.

From the 1860s, virtually all the Jewish merchants of Essaouira were protégés, and a few had even acquired foreign nationality. Backed by the foreign powers, Jewish protégés were increasingly pressing their claims in the rural countryside. Economic problems were exacerbated during this period by drought and famine, which led to the expropriation of rural lands—certainly one cause of the increasing alienation of peasants from the land.[65] Rural vagrants, often associated with the brigands of Haha or Shiadma, roamed the town. The rural caids began to pressure the governor of Essaouira to obtain the release of their fellow tribesmen imprisoned in the town.[66]

Inasmuch as foreign intervention added to the severity of Moroccan economic problems and caused increasing tensions between town and country, disputes between Muslims and Jews grew, making Jews more vulnerable to attack. In January 1872, for example, rural dwellers came to town during the *'āshūrā'* celebration, broke into houses, and insulted Jews. The local authorities were unable to prevent the affray.[67] In 1883, the authorities canceled the *'āshūrā'* celebrations because of pressures from the French consular agent, who had probably been influenced by the urgings of Jewish protégés. The British consul wrote to the Jewish community requesting that they abstain from interfering with the local officials on this issue. Tensions between Muslims and Jews increased in the Bazaar. Jewish protégés disciplined by the *muḥtasib* invoked their consular representatives on their own invoked their consular representatives on their own behalf.[68]

The Violation of Ethnic Boundaries

Ethnic boundaries, therefore, were being redefined as foreign intervention increased. From the 1870s on, the spatial divisions in the town between Muslim and Jew were being redefined by Jewish protégés. In the crisis of overcrowding, the Jewish merchants for the first time began to acquire houses in the medina. The commercial activities of Akkan Corcos, for example, began to interfere with a mosque, because various pack animals and caravans were cluttering the street. The sultan was alerted to the incident, and the legal authorities of the town were asked to take measures.[69] In 1885, a Frenchman opened up a public bath *(ḥammām)*, frequented by Christians and Jews, in the medina. Public premises such as *ḥammām*s generally belonged to the *habous*, and the action by the French subject was clearly seen as a violation of the Muslim private realm. The person who had mortgaged the property of the bath was arrested by the authorities, though the *ḥammām* continued to operate. Meyer Corcos then constructed a *ḥammām* of his own in the mellah; the authorities interfered and had the construction workers flogged.[70] In a sense, the construction of these *ḥammāms* was regarded as a violation against the sovereignty of the Islamic state: the sultan regarded the *ḥammāms* as Muslim public edifices that properly belonged under the control of the *habous* administration.[71]

These incidents reinforced a general feeling that Jewish protégés were challenging the system. They increasingly began to acquire *habous* property, and as a consequence, the foreign consulates, in representing them, became enmeshed in bitter disputes with the *habous* adminstration. For example, a Jewish protégé in 1872 rented some shops from the *habous*. To the dismay of the authorities, the direction of prayer *(qibla)* of the adjacent mosque faced these shops, which were to be occupied by a Jew.[72] This foreign-backed invasion of Muslim space was perceived as a growing threat to the social order. Protégés began to speculate in low-rent *habous* property by purchasing the key rights *(miftāḥ)* and then subletting their holdings at a sizable profit. In 1877, the sultan ordered the authorities in Essaouira to prevent *habous* property from being appropriated by protégés in auctions.[73] The sultan's decree failed to prevent this kind of speculation, which was clearly to the detriment of the Muslim poor. In 1887, the keeper of the *habous* *(nāẓir al-aḥbās)* in Essaouira asked for a royal *dahir* to abolish the practice of subletting premises of the *habous* at a profit.[74]

While these conflicts were certainly real, they were undoubtedly blown out of proportion because of the political conflict between Morocco and the foreign powers. Every minor incident adopted as a cause célèbre by the Alliance Israélite Universelle or the Anglo-Jewish Association had diplomatic repercussions, reverberating in the Foreign Office and the Quai d'Orsay. Instead of turning to the Muslim authorities to regulate the problems, the protégés immediately approached the foreign consulates.[75] The system of mediating disputes through the intercession of sultan or *sīd* was now being replaced by intervention of foreign consulates.

Conclusions

The task of interpreting Muslim-Jewish relations in precolonial Morocco is complicated because of the large amount of diplomatic correspondence relating to conflicts between Jewish protégés and the Muslim authorities. These disputes are found reproduced in the consular archives of all the foreign powers and the official correspondence of the makhzan. The impression left by these tomes of correspondence is that Jewish-Muslim relations had significantly deteriorated. But in a wider context, the period preceding the establishment of the French protectorate in 1912 was a time of general political and social turmoil. Tensions and conflicts were magnified by strife between various social groups: Jews and Muslims, townsmen and tribesmen, and government officials and taxpayers. What is also significant is that despite this instability, cordial market relations between Jews and Muslims prevailed. Despite the partial undermining of the *dhimma* pact system, the market continued to function as a mediating influence on a day-to-day basis. Parallel to the growth of disorder and irregularities was the increasing interdependency of Muslim and Jew. New distribution networks brought Jews into new markets. Town and country were still linked by the ubiquitous Jewish peddler. With the establishment of the French protectorate, new roads and truck transport gave the itinerant trader new opportunities. The patron-client relations between Jew and Muslim, between the itinerant Jewish trader and his *sīd*, were maintained until the 1950s.

In 1906 Morocco was in a state of political anarchy, as supporters of 'Abd al-'Azīz struggled with supporters of 'Abd al-Ḥāfiẓ over the future of the throne.[76] The town of Essaouira itself was under seige by a tribal rebel, Qā'id Anflūs, who supported the 'Azīzist cause. For ten days the caid and his tribesmen occupied the town. Popular discontent erupted, and the houses of the mellah facing the main street were vandalized by a mob of rural and urban poor. The Jews barricaded themselves behind the closed gates of the mellah, and the mob ransacked some of the shops in town. Anflūs, calling for an end to Muslim-Jewish intermingling, then had those Jews who had acquired homes in the medina expelled and sent back to the mellah. (Apparently, Jews had been moving into the medina in increasing numbers in the preceding years.) An estimated 200 families were compelled to return to the mellah.[77] Jews of Essaouira recount how the various Jewish distilleries of eau-de-vie *(maḥya)* in the medina were closed down. With the arrival of a French cruiser followed by a contingent of Moroccan troops, Anflūs and his tribesmen left the town and order was restored. The Muslim authorities decided that it was probably better to keep the Jews out of the medina—the need to restore ethnic boundaries as expressed by physical space was clearly felt. Yet the authorities made sure that the Jewish distilleries of the mellah were reopened. The prevalence of *maḥya* distilleries was not only to meet the needs of Jewish consumption: Jews had historically been the suppliers of alcoholic beverages to the Muslims. The director of the Alliance Israélite Universelle writes in dismay about the moral effect of the disturbances: "Jews and Arabs have always fraternized at Mogador. . . . Never anti-Semitism, never the shadow of religous persecutions." Muslim-Jewish relations, temporarily disrupted by the invasion of Anflūs, were restored to a modus vivendi—the maintenance of ethnic spatial barriers together with the interchange of business and commercial relations.

This system was maintained until the mass exodus of Jews from southwestern Morocco in the late 1950s and early 1960s. The Muslims today look back nostalgically to the days when the ambulent Jewish peddler circulated in the countryside. In the town of Essaouira, the economic eclipse of the town is attributed to the departure of the Jews. In recent Moroccan parliamentary elections, a Jewish businessman from Meknes was popularly elected as deputy for Essaouira by the town's almost entirely Muslim population.[78] It appears to reflect the belief that Jewish business acumen might still have the chance to restore the prosperity of Essaouira.

ABBREVIATIONS

A.E.	Archives du Ministère des Affaires Etrangères, Paris.
A.I.U.	Archives de l'Alliance Israélite Universelle, Paris.
B.A.	Bayrūk Archives, documents of the Bayrūk family, Goulimine.
B.D.	Archives of the Bū Damī'a family, Iligh, Tazarwalt.
C.A.	Corcos Archives, documents of the Corcos family, Jerusalem.
D.A.R.	Direction des Archives Royales, Rabat.
F.O.	Records of the Foreign Office, Public Record Office, London.
K.H.	al-Khizānat al-Ḥasaniyya, Royal Palace, Rabat.
N.A.	National Archives, Diplomatic Branch, Washington, D.C.

NOTES

1. The present study is based in part on chapters 4 and 5 of my book, *Merchants of Essaouira: Urban Society and Imperialism in Southwestern Morocco, 1844–1886* (Cambridge, 1988). I would like to thank Peter von Sivers for his comments on this paper, and Shlomo Lederman for his remarks on the Hebrew translations.

2. On Morocco, see Clifford Geertz, "Suq: The Bazaar Economy of Sefrou," in Clifford Geertz, Hildred Geertz, and Lawrence Rosen, *Meaning and Order in Moroccan Society* (Cambridge, 1979), 133–40; Lawrence Rosen, *Bargaining for Reality: The Construction of Social Relations in a Muslim Community*

(Chicago, 1984), pp. 148–63; K. L. Brown, "Mellah and Medina: A Moroccan City and Its Jewish Quarters (Salé ca. 1880–1930)," in *Studies in Judaism and Islam*, ed. Shlomo Morag et al. (Jerusalem, 1981), pp. 266–76; Dale F. Eickelman, "Religion and Trade in Western Morocco," *Research in Economic Anthropology* 5 (1983): 336–41. Other parts of North Africa have also been studied. See Abraham L. Udovitch and Lucette Valensi, *The Last Arab Jews: The Communities of Jerba, Tunisia* (London, 1984), pp. 101–6; Harvey Goldberg, ed., *The Book of Mordechai: A Study of the Jews in Libya* (Philadelphia, 1980), pp. 77–80.

3. See, for example, the study of Aḥmad Tawfīq, *al-Mujtama' al-Maghribī fī 'l-qarn at-tāsi' 'ashr: Īnūltān (1850–1912)* (Rabat, 1978), pp. 304–13; idem, "Les juifs dans la société marocain au 19e siècle: l'exemple des juifs de Demnat," in *Juifs du Maroc, identité et dialogue* (Grenoble, 1980), pp. 153–66. For a general discussion on ways that foreign intervention disturbed Muslim-Jewish relations, see the comprehensive bibliographical essay of Mohammad Kenbib, "Les relations entre musulmans et juifs au Maroc 1859–1945," *Hespéris Tamuda* 23 (1985): 83–104.

4. Michael M. Laskier, *The Alliance Israélite Universelle and the Jewish Communities of Morocco, 1862–1962* (Albany, N.Y., 1983), pp. 34ff. For more general discussion, see Bernard Lewis, *The Jews of Islam* (Princeton, 1984), pp. 154ff.; Norman A. Stillman, *The Jews of Arab lands* (Philadelphia, 1979), pp. 95–107.

5. On the history of the mellahs in Morocco, see David Corcos, *Studies in the History of the Jews of Morocco* (Jerusalem, 1976), pp. 64–130; Stillman, *Jews of Arab Lands*, pp. 79–81.

6. In 1864, the makhzan was considering a plan to extend the area of the mellah in Essaouira. The problem with the proposed site, as the vizier Bū 'Ashrīn indicates in a letter to Abraham and Jacob Corcos, was that the proposed site was "inhabited and filled with people from the Shabānāt, but moreover, there is a mosque in it and it would be inappropriate to add it [the site] to the mellah for construction since the mosque would then be in its [i.e., the mellah's] midst." C.A., 14 Ramaḍān 1280/22 February 1864. The proximity of synagogues to mosques was a cause of friction between Jews and Muslims in sixteenth-century Jerusalem, as the Jewish community increased in size. Cf. Amnon Cohen, *Jewish Life Under Islam: Jerusalem in the Sixteenth Century* (Cambridge, Mass., 1984), pp. 76–86.

7. Cf. André Raymond, *Grandes villes arabes à l'époque ottomane* (Paris, 1985), pp. 295–98.

8. The mellahs of southern Morocco were studied by Pierre Flamand just prior to the departure of the Jews. *Diaspora en terre d'Islam: les communautés israélites du sud marocain* (Casablanca, n.d. [1959]).

9. Raymond, *Grandes villes*, pp. 172–74.

10. Auguste Beaumier, "Mogador et son commerce maritime," *Annales du Commerce Extérieur*, Etats-Barbaresques, faits commerciaux, 17 (1875): 118.

11. Cf. Corcos, *Jews of Morocco*, pp. 120–23. For Salé, cf. Brown, "Mellah

and Medina," pp. 254–56. An original letter dated 1807 concerning Sulaymān's order is edited in Dawid 'Obadiya, *Qehīllat Ṣefrū* (Jerusalem, 1975), vol. 1, p. 35. The British consular agent in Essaouira reports that initially the sultan was going to allow the Jews two years to retain their houses until they built new ones in the mellah, but he was angered by their demands and ordered them to relocate immediately. F.O., 174/13, 30 June 1807, Gwyn to Green.

12. Yiṣḥaq Ben Ya'īsh Halewī, *Hasfīrah*, 86 (1891): 1129.

13. Descriptive accounts are found in Budgett Meakin, *The Land of the Moors* (London, 1901), p. 212; C. Ollive, "Géographie médicale: climat de Mogador et de son influence sur la phthisie," *Bulletin de la Société de Géographie* (Paris), 6th Ser., 10 (1875): 372.

14. Cf. Udovitch and Valensi, *Last Arab Jews*, pp. 64–66.

15. Halewī, *Hasfīrah* 76 (1891), 311.

16. See Norman A. Stillman, "Some Notes on the Judeo-Arabic Dialect of Sefrou (Morocco), in *Studies in Judaism and Islam*, ed. Morag et al., pp. 231–51. Cf. Goldberg, *Book of Mordechai*, pp. 79–80. Information about Iligh and its Jewish community is derived from fieldwork in Iligh in 1981, and from interviews with Ilighi Jews in Marrakesh, Inzegan, Casablanca, and Israel that same year. I have not been able to determine when, if ever, the Jews of Iligh spoke Berber as their primary language. As early as the first decade of the nineteenth century, legal statements by Jews in the register book of the sharif Hāshim of Iligh are signed in Judeo-Arabic. B.D., *kunnāsh* 2.

17. From an exhaustive list of all the *habous* property in Essaouira established by the French protectorate authorities after 1913 it has been estimated that 26.6 percent were rented by Jews, though they paid about 41.5 percent of the total rent. However, seven out of ten of the biggest *habous* holders were Jews. Thomas K. Park, "Administration and the Economy: Morocco 1880 to 1980. The Case of Essaouira" (Ph.D. diss., University of Wisconsin, 1983), pp. 492–94.

18. Halewī, *Hasfīrah* 143 (1891): 581.

19. *Jewish Missionary Intelligence* 21 (August 1905): 117.

20. There has been considerable discussion on patron-client relations between Muslim and Jew in Morocco. See, for example, Geertz, "Suq," pp. 137–38; Brown, "Mellah and Medina," pp. 268–70; Rosen, *Bargaining for Reality*, pp. 136–37; Allan R. Myers," in *Jewish Societies in the Middle East*, ed. Shlomo Deshen and Walter P. Zenner (Washington, D.C., 1982), pp. 85–104; Moshe Shokeid, "Jewish Existence in a Berber Environment," in *Jewish Societies*, ed. Deshen and Zenner, pp. 105–22.

21. A.I.U., Maroc XXXIV E 588, 13 June 1902, Bensimhon.

22. A.I.U., Maroc XXXVII bis E b.

23. On the return of itinerant Jewish peddlers for the festivals, cf. Geertz, "Suq," pp. 171, 250, n. 87. On the Jews of Todgha, cf. Haïm Zafrani, *Pédagogie juive en terre d'Islam* (Paris, 1969), p. 35.

24. K.H., K[122]

25. This has been studied in a monograph by Edward Westermarck, *Ceremonies and Beliefs Connected with Agriculture, Certain Dates of the Solar Year, and the Weather in Morocco* (Helsinki, 1913); cf. Jacques Berque, *Structures sociales du Haut-Atlas*, 2d ed. (Paris, 1978), pp. 130–34, 276–79.

26. E.g., Mordekhai Rbībō of the mellah of Ifrane received from Husayn Hāshim, the sharif of Iligh, the sum of 1,257 riyal in credit on 28 Dhū al-Ḥijja 1291 (5 February 1875), so that he could buy ostrich feathers. The document certifies that "repayment of what he owed has been deferred until the coming *moussem* of March (*mārs*), God willing." The cycle continues the following year. On 6 November 1876, Rbībō receives credit to purchase feathers. It was to be repaid at the March *moussem*. B.D., K[10], 20–3, 21–1.

27. The commerce of Tazarwalt, organized and protected by the *shurfa* of Iligh has been closely studied by Paul Pascon, "Le commerce de la maison d'lligh d'après le registre comptable de Husayn b. Hachem: Tazerwalt 1850–1875," in Paul Pascon et al., *La Maison d' Iligh et l'histoire sociale du Tazerwalt* (Rabat, 1984), pp. 43–90.

28. Ibid., p. 81 n. 37.

29. Most estimates of the Jewish population of Iligh in the nineteenth century by foreign travelers seem to be exaggerated, according to our study of the estimated mortality rate reflected in the Jewish cemetery. In about 1870 when the economic strength of Iligh was at its height, we have estimated that the Jewish community contained about 500 persons. In the early 1880s, after a period of severe drought, the population was reduced to about 300. Paul Pascon and Daniel Schroeter, "Le cimetière juif d'Iligh 1751–1955: étude des épitaphes comme documents d'historie démographique," in Pascon, *La Maison d'Iligh*, pp. 123–24, 134–38.

30. A. I. U., Maroc XXVII bis E 6.

31. Letter of 14 August 1884, Mahon, in Jean-Louis Miège, *Documents d'histoire économique et sociale marocaine au xixe siècle* (Paris, 1969), p. 174.

32. The royal merchants of Essaouira have been studied by Jean-Louis Miège, *Le Maroc et l'Europe, 1830–1894* (Paris, 1961–62), vol. 2, pp. 92–94; cf. Michel Abitbol, *Temoins et acteurs: les Corcos et l'histoire du Maroc contemporain* (Jerusalem, 1977), pp. 20–28.

33. An example is the case of a merchant who had to leave a guarantor before traveling to London to recover the inheritance after the death of his brother there. His guarantor was delegated to pay his monthly installment to the makhzan until his return. D. A. R., Essaouira 1, 24 Ramaḍān 1270/20 June 1854, Muḥammad Brīsha to Sultan Muḥammad IV.

34. B. D., Correspondance Politique, 29 Ṣafar 1262/26 February 1846, Muhammad Bū Mah[dī] to Ḥusayn b. Hāshim [these letters are translated in French in a forthcoming posthumous publication of Paul Pascon].

35. Apparently the *nazāla* was an old term. See the comments by ʻAbd al-Wahhāb Ibn Manṣūr, *al-Wathā'iq* 4 (1978): 378. For nineteenth-century

descriptions of *nazālas*, see Arthur Leared, *Marocco and the Moors* (London, 1876), p. 103; J. D. Hooker and J. Ball, *Journal of a Tour in Morocco and the Great Atlas* (London, 1878), p. 110; A. Marcet, *Le Maroc: Voyage d'une mission française à la cour du Sultan* (Paris, 1885), p. 233; Halewī, *Hasfīrah* 145 (1891): 589; Hubert Gíraud, "Itinéraire de Mogador à Marrakech (1890–92)," *C. R. de Séances du Congrès National de Géographie, Marseille* (1898): 4. A case is reported in 1874 of a small party of Jews killed at a *nazāla* in Shiadma. A. I. U., Maroc XXXIII E 571, 25 December 1874, Emile Altaras.

36. Cf. Geertz, "Suq," pp. 137–38.

37. Ibid.; Brown, "Mellah and Medina," p. 269.

38. Edward Westermarck, *Ritual and Belief in Morocco* (London, 1926), vol. I, p. 535. Westermarck mistakenly leads us to believe that *al-'ār* implied "curse" and "sin." It has been shown that its usage related to "honor" and "shame." See K. L. Brown, "The 'Curse' of Westermarck," *Acta Philsophica Fennica* 34 (1982): 219–59.

39. This system was noted by nineteenth-century observers, e.g., Charles de Foucauld, *Reconnaissance au Maroc* (Paris, 1888), pp. 130–32; Walter B. Harris, *Tafilet: The Narrative of a Journey of Exploration in the Atlas Mountains and the Oases of the North-West Sahara* (London, 1985), pp. 98–99. Halewī, *Hasfīrah* 71 (1892): 289; and it has been studied more recently by Raymond Jamous, *Honneur et baraka: les structures sociales traditionnelles dans le Rif* (Cambridge, 1981), pp. 212–16. It has been suggested that the killing of a Jew was regarded as a worse offense than killing a Muslim, since Jews generally were not part of the political system and the patron would retaliate with little mercy. David M. Hart, *The Aith Waryaghar of the Moroccan Rif* (Tucson, Ariz., 1976), p. 280; cf. Rosen, *Bargaining for Reality*, p. 153.

40. A.E., C.C.C., Mogador 6, 18 August 1879, Hélouis. See the discussion of Pascon, *La Maison d'Iligh*, pp. 83–90.

41. Cf. Meyers, "Patronage and Protection," pp. 93–94.

42. This has been remarked by nineteenth-century observers, e.g., Arthur de Capell Brooke, *Sketches in Spain and Morocco* (London, 1831), pp. 251–53; E. M. Stutfield, *El Maghreb, 1200 Miles' Ride Through Morocco* (London, 1886), p. 277.

43. See the remarks of Ernest Gellner, *Saints of the Atlas* (Chicago, 1969), pp. 22–29.

44. The documents from the archives of Iligh confirm this situation reported by our informants. B.D., 5 Ramaḍān 1305/7 June 1886, Sultan al-Ḥasan to Ḥusayn ū Hāshim. Foreign travelers noted that Jews were considered to be the personal property of the chiefs, and were compelled to leave their families behind as hostages when they traveled, e.g., M. Quedenfeldt, *Division et répartion de la population berbère au Maroc* (Algiers, 1904), pp. 63–64.

45. Halewī, *Hasfīrah*, 141 (1891): 141.

46. The French consul of Essaouira reports that Ḥusayn of Iligh saved a small Jewish community on the former's request. A.I.U., France VIII D 42, 22 April 1874, Beaumier to Crémieux.

47. The *qirāḍ*-type agreement existed since the Middle Ages; see Abraham L. Udovitch, *Partnership and Profit in Medieval Islam* (Princeton, 1970), pp. 170ff. Cf. Geertz, "Suq," pp. 133–34.

48. E.g., Mas'ūd 'Amār and his father of Ifrane traded on the capital of the Corcos house while obtaining loans from Ḥusayn ū Hāshim of Iligh. B.D., K[3], fols. 163[1], 163[2], 18 Jumāda I 1279/11 November 1862; C.A., 5 Nīssan 5623/25 March 1863, commenda contract drawn up by two *dayyans* of Essaouira, Abraham b. Ya'aqōb Ben 'Aṭṭār and Mōshe Hakōhen. The agreement is between Mas'ūd 'Amār and Abraham Corcos.

49. One of the principal Muslim royal merchants of Essaouira, Mukhtār b. 'Azūz employed Jewish commission agents. K.H., 15 Rabī' II 1281/17 September 1864, al-Mahdī b. al-Mashāwrī to Ibrāhīm b. Sa'īd.

50. Examples of this are found in the Corcos archives. E.g., C.A. 24 Rajab 1290/17 September 1873, 'Abd al-Mālik Ibn 'Abdallāh ū Bīhī to Abraham Corcos; 1 Dhū al-Ḥijja 1285/15 March 1869, Aḥmad b. Muḥammad as-Sūsī al-Waltītī aṣ-Ṣawīrī to Abraham Corcos. Reuben Elmaleh loaned money to Daḥmān Bayrūk. B.A., 26 Shawwāl 1311/2 May 1894.

51. A letter to Solomon Corcos from a rural caid in 1850 alludes to some good allegedly lost. It would be unacceptable, according to this letter, that goods which Corcos confided "in God's protection *[fī amān Allāh]*" could be lost. C.A., 25 Muḥarram 1267/30 November 1850.

52. There is a legend of the venerated rabbi of Essaouira, Hayyīm Pīnṭō being carried out of town by Rabbi Haddān, finding sanctuary at the residence of the powerful caid 'Abdallāh ū Bīhī. Abraham Ben 'Aṭṭār, *Shannōt Ḥayyīm* (Casablanca, 1958), p. 4. Abraham Corcos and his pregnant wife, Miryam, found refuge with Muḥammad ū Mūbārak south of the town. In the village of Kouzimt, their son Meyer was born. C.A., Judeo-Arabic diary of Meyer Corcos.

53. N.A., R.G. 84, Mogador, 15 January 1888, Meyer Corcos to W. Reed.

54. The archives of the Bayrūk family are currently being studied by Mustapha Naïmi. See his article: "La politique des chefs de la confederation Tekna face à l'expansionnisme commercial européen," *Revue d'Histoire Maghrebine* 11 (1984): 153–73.

55. Abraham Laredo, *Les noms des juifs du Maroc* (Madrid, 1978), pp. 359–60. The commodities in which the Afriats dealt in Essaouira can be inferred from the customs duties registers of the port. K.H., K[46] 1279/1862–63; K[120] 1301/1883.

56. Pascon, *La Maison d'Iligh*, pp. 76–77.

57. On the revolt of Bū Iḥlās, see Muḥammad al-Mukhtār as-Sūsī, *al-Ma'sūl* (Casablanca, 1960–61), vol. 5, pp. 142–44. In the tradition of the Jews of Essaouira, fifty Jews of Ifrane were burned by rebels. Consequently, the community of Ifrane moved to other towns and regions, such as Aït Baha and Essaouira. Cf. V. Monteil, "Les Juifs d'Ifrane," *Hespéris* 35 (1948): 154–55; Corcos, *Jews of Morocco*, pp. 117–18; Pierre Flamand, *Quelques manifestations de l'esprit populaires dans les juiveries du Sud-Marocain* (Casablanca, 1959), pp.

23–32. Evidence for the vibrancy of the Jewish community of Ifrane is found in the account books of Iligh. Pascon, *La Maison d'Iligh*, p. 81.

58. Halewī reports that three mellahs had been established there seventy years previously. (i.e., ca. 1820). *Hasfīrah* 67 (1891): 268.

59. Halewī, *Hasfīrah* 81 (1891): 331. On the Jewish population in the general region of Essaouira, see *Jewish Missionary Intelligence* 15 (September 1899): 139–40; (October 1899): 150–54. The places in Haha and Shiadma known to have had mellahs are Had Dra'a, Tlata, Hanshan, Sidi Mukhtar, Meskalla, Smimou, and Kouzimt. Thomas Park and I have investigated these mellahs, but have found no clear data regarding their origins.

60. The subject of "protection" has been the focus of much research on precolonial Morocco, and several monographs have been written on the subject: E. F. Cruickshank, *Morocco at the Parting of the Ways* (Philadelphia, 1935); Leland L. Bowie, "The Protégé System in Morocco: 1880–1904" (Ph.D. diss., University of Michigan, 1970); 'Abd al-Wahhāb Ibn Manṣūr, *Mushkilat al-ḥimayāt al-qunṣilīya bi-l-Maghrib* (Rabat, 1977); Mohamed Kenbib, "Les protections étrangères au Maroc aux XIXème siècle—début du XXème," (Paris VII, 1980).

61. I have attempted to reconstruct some of the events of the revolt and its effect on Essaouira in my book *Merchants of Essaouira*, pp. 182–84.

62. A.I.U., France VIII D 42, 31 January 1875, Beaumier to Crémieux.

63. A number of responses to the sultan's decree are found in the archives: D.A.R., Yahūd, 18 Ṣafar 1303/26 November 1885, 25 Ṣafar 1303/3 December 1885, Būshtā b. al-Baghdādī; 26 Ṣafar 1303/4 December 1885, Muḥammad b. [Hammu] ad-Dimnātī, 28 Ṣafar 1303/6 December 1885, al-'Arabī [——], 29 Ṣafar 1303/7 December 1885, 'Abd ar-Raḥmān Lubarūs, 15 Rabī' I 1303/2 December 1885, Muḥammad b. Aḥmad al-Khadar. The dahir sent to Qadi Ḥamīd Banānī of Essaouira is found in Aḥmad Ibn al-Ḥājj, *Durar al-jawhariyya fī madḥ al-khilāfat al-Ḥasaniyya*, K.H., MS 512, vol. II (fol. not enumerated).

64. D.A.R., Essaouira 3, 28 Rajab 1292/30 August 1875, 20 Dhū al-Qa'da 1292/18 December 1875, Sultan to 'Amāra. This concerns a case of a trader who refused to pay the tax on a consignment of ostrich feathers. The feathers, according to the governor of Essaouira, were stored at Wad Noun for two years until Abraham Afriat and Messan Knaffo, wealthy protégés and natives of Goulimine, arranged to have them conveyed to Essaouira under the guise of their protégé status. Cf. Kenbib, "Les protections étrangères," pp. 185–86.

65. There is a considerable amount of administrative correspondence between Essaouira and the Palace regarding this issue in the 1870s and 1880s. See the discussion in Schroeter, "Merchants and Pedlars," pp. 404–409.

66. Ibid., pp. 371–72.

67. F.O., 631/5, 12 January 1872, Carstensen to Hay.

68. These incidents are reported by the British consul Payton in Essaouira. F.O., 174/292, 2 November 1883, 6 November 1883, 9 November 1883, 12 November 1883, 20 November 1883.

69. D.A.R.., 5 Muḥarram 1292/11 February 1875, Sultan al-Hasan to the caid 'Amāra.

70. N.A., R.G. 84, Mogador, 5 February 1885, 9 February 1885, 24 March 1885, 24 April 1885, 12 June 1885, Corcos to Mathews; 28 Rabī' I 1302/15 January 1885 Dawbilālī (the caid of Essaouira) to Corcos.

71. D.A.R., 20 Rabī II 1302/6 February 1885, Muḥammad b. 'Abd ar-Raḥmān Brīsha, Muḥammad b. Zākūr, 'Abd ar-Raḥmān b. al-Ḥasan to Sultan al-Ḥasan.

72. D.A.R., Jumādā II 1289, 27 Jumādā II 1289/1 September 1872, 'Amāra to Bargāsh.

73. D.A.R., 'Amāra, 11 Ramaḍān 1894/19 September 1877, Sultan al-Ḥasan to 'Amāra.

74. B.H., 10 Ṣafar 1305/28 October 1887, al-Ḥabīb as-Sarrār to Sultan al-Ḥasan.

75. For Demnat, cf. Tawfīq, "Les juifs," pp. 157–64.

76. Edmund Burke, *Prelude to Protectorate in Morocco* (Chicago, 1976), pp. 99ff.

77. A.I.U., Maroc XXXIII E 582, 2 September 1906, 9 September 1906, 12 September 1906, Benchimol; A.I.U., Maroc III C 10, 2 September 1906, 6 September 1906, C. Taurel; *Jewish Missionary Intelligence* 22 (December 1906): 183; *Al-Moghreb El-Aqsa*, 15 September 1906, 22 September 1906, 29 September 1906.

78. Paul Balta, "Essaouira, ville-décor," *Le Monde*, 4–5 November 1984.

DATE DUE

DEC 31 '02 S			
DEC 17 2002			
GAYLORD			PRINTED IN U.S.A.